1

CAUGHT UP in the FABLE

A Tale of Rock and Roll

CAUGHT UP in the FABLE

A Tale of Rock and Roll

By John Diaz and Neil Feineman

As you get older, you realize that the past, like beauty, resides increasingly in the eyes of the beholder. I have done my best to depict these stories as truthfully and as objectively as I can. Other people may recall situations and events slightly differently ~ that's just the way it works. My hope is that there is more common ground to these varied versions than not, because at the end of the day, we're all groping the same elephant, whether we like it or not.

Dedicated always and forever too....
Nancy Louise

The Birds and the bees
The flowers and the trees
The moon up above
And a thing called love*

*With thanks and credit to Herb Newman

PROLOGUE

We huddle on the tarmac in various states of shock and injury. The wind causes the rain to blow sideways rather than from above, so that it slices into you. Be it from the wind or an injury, I can barely stand up.

No one else is in sight, so, alone in the dark, wind and rain, we can't help but feel that we're the only people left alive. The seven of us, stunned, stare at the broken body of the 747, a few hundred feet away from us. Now fully aflame, explosions shoot out of the fuselage, sending streaks of fire hundreds of feet in the air. The smell of burning jet fuel is overpowering, as is the tremendous heat from the wreckage. The wing on the side of the plane facing us has snapped off almost at the fuselage. The other wing tilts wildly up to the sky like a gigantic, fiery finger. The door, which just seconds ago provided our avenue of escape, now spews fire like a flamethrower.

Everything moves in slow motion. The rain, which is falling in sheets, cascades towards, and then past, my eyes. The flames from the hulking mass undulate like waves of multi-colored grain in a stiff wind. Sparks fly upwards, leaving distinctive trails into the pitch-black sky.

I check myself out, and then my surroundings. Although my body feels numb, I am still upright. I clutch my carry-on, which I had grabbed on the mad dash out of the plane, tightly to my body. My knuckles wrap around the leather casing, a pale white save for the blue spider-webbed veins traversing them. I am detached, outside my corporeal self, as if I am an observer, not a player, in the scene.

Struck dumb, no one has yet spoken. We don't have to. Fear, relief, pain, sadness and other emotions flicker across faces like words appearing in one of those magic eight balls that I use to be so infatuated with when I was a kid. Everyone, including myself, is glowing strangely in a beautiful white/blue flicker. I can't tell if that is an effect from the mixture of rain, fire and jet fuel or a remnant of the crash.

I think I'm the first one to speak. My voice sounds far away, and I realize my hearing has been suspended due to the explosions or stress. I ask if everyone is OK and get varying answers as we all start to take stock of our physical beings. Then I wonder out loud when is someone going to come and help us.

I retrieve my cell phone from my bag, call my dad in New Orleans and tell him I'm okay. Next I call my wife, Nancy, who is still asleep in California. At first she thinks I'm teasing. As soon as she realizes I'm not, she breaks down.

Finally, I notice distant lights, hopefully of an emergency vehicle, coming towards us from the terminal. Although it has been just minutes, it feels as if we have been standing there for hours. The wind and rain continue to wail tremendously. Standing is increasingly difficult. I notice a high pitch whine in my ears and I continually cough up black phlegm. My entire body is sore. I feel like I'm going to collapse.

At last, the emergency vehicle finally arrives. The glow from the flashing lights ripples through the rain and across the wet tarmac. The driver babbles unintelligibly to most of us, in either Cantonese or Mandarin. He is flustered and doesn't know what to do. Somehow, we convince him to get us off the runway and into the terminal.

As we pile in and speed back to the terminal, I realize that I have survived a plane crash. I watched many die gruesomely in front of me, and I wonder again if we seven are the only survivors. I also realize that from this moment on, nothing will ever be the same for me. For part of me will always be in Taiwan, on a rain-soaked tarmac at Chiang Kai Shek Airport, on Halloween night, the 31st of October, in the year 2000.

Prologue *Re-dux*

I am ushered into a crowded eight by thirteen foot prison cell with 33 other grown men. There are six bunks in the cell, so every inch of floor space is taken up with bodies so tightly packed together that you can't get to the small, open bathroom without treading on someone every few steps. I am given the bottom of a three-tiered, six foot long by 30-inch wide metal bunk bed that I get to share with a gangbanger named Pelon. We lay in opposite directions, socked feet in each other's face. It is the middle of the night.

Most of the others are sleeping, except for a few junkies going through the agony of cold-turkey withdrawal, who are either curled up in balls and whimpering on the floor or noisily retching into the non-flushable cement hole that passes for a toilet. I notice that no light emanates from anyone in that cell, including myself.

The cell is in a holding area. After 72 hours, you either are released on bail or processed into the general population of the prison. I'd like to think that all will go well, but just the fact that I'm here makes me think otherwise.

The problem started four days ago, when I was grabbed by the Tijuana Police, literally right off the street. I had just gone to a doctor and then a pharmacy, and filled a prescription for a muscle relaxer called SOMA. My wife and my doctors in the US had no idea I was doing this. In fact, everyone thought I was in San Diego, and didn't even know I was in Mexico. I spent the first three days in a cell in a building that housed the Mexican District attorneys, accused, as I learned from an American Embassy official, of buying drugs with the intent to distribute (sell) them. The official was also quick to point out that I most probably was shit out of luck.

In Mexico, he explained, I was guilty until proven innocent of intent to distribute drugs. I was facing up to ten years in prison, and, as my representative, he was here to tell me that there was nothing the US government could do to help.

He did recommend that I call one of the attorneys on the list he had given me, and that I learn Spanish, which would be useful in prison. This was the first and last time I was to see a representative of the US government throughout my ordeal.

After three days, when negotiations for my release at the border between my friends and representatives of the Tijuana police, had broken down, they moved me here, to the infamous La Mesa Penitentiary, nicknamed *La Pinta*, or the Pint, located some 20 kilometers from the Tijuana border, to await trial. That, they told me, could take up to a year. As soon as I was alone, I tried to choke myself to death with my T-shirt. Somehow, I even managed to bungle that.

So once again, I am spending Halloween in a foreign country. Only this time, I'm in prison. It is October 31st, 2010. My nightmare has just begun.

PART ONE

My Life in the Music Industry

Rock N' Roll

You hit the road
Or the road hits back at you
Either way,
You wind up black and blue
Tarred head to foot
Life's oily residue
Sisyphus pushes that rock
N' rolls it all over you

How did it ever get to this? I mean, I understand intellectually and physically how I ended up in one of the most notorious prisons in Mexico. This is about as redundant as redundancy gets, as Mexico is known for its notorious prisons, but, philosophically, it is extremely hard for me to rationalize.

Nothing, it would seem to me, in my life should have brought me to this evil place. I should have realized by now, my 60th year on the planet, with all that has transpired before this seemingly incongruous situation, that life follows no predictable paths and the future is always unknown, ever unfolding in ways that one can never predict. It hardly seems plausible that a career that started in Woodstock, in the summer of love, would end up some 40 years later in one of Mexico's prisons.

Nonetheless, here I am, with little more than the lyrics of an old Kingston Trio song, "Tijuana Jail," ("So here we are in the Tijuana jail/Ain't got no friends to go our bail/So here we'll stay 'cause we can't pay/Just send our mail to the Tijuana jail") running through my head.

Unlike the catchy folk hit that I listened to on my transistor radio so long ago, however, the song sounds like a funeral dirge to me. As well it should, since every second I spend in this hellish hole puts not just my life, but my very soul, in danger.

I'm here, of course, because of drugs. Drugs that were prescribed to me and drugs I prescribed to myself. Drugs that were fed to me by doctors trying to combat the injuries from a plane crash, that has left me in constant pain and mental agony for ten years. And drugs I fed myself, simply because they made me feel good.

The contrast between then and now is almost too much to bear. Before, I lived life like a rock star, with the great cities of the world as my playground. Now, everything in my life is a lesson in humility. I share a cell with nine other men. I witness nonchalant human rights abuses that a silver spooned guy like myself could not have imagined. I spend all day walking myself into hallucinatory trances that undermine my sanity. I wait, day after day, for some news about my fate. And, as if my life were a movie, I lose myself in my past, when I, like rock 'n' roll, was still young.

1969
By the time I got to Woodstock...

In the summer of 1969, I was 19. My parents were well off, so instead of having to find a menial summer job, I spent the summer hanging out in the offices of the producers of the upcoming New Orleans Pop Festival, as a glorified, unpaid intern.

My biggest concern of the moment was impressing this girl I was interested in. (This, being rock and roll, there was always a girl). She was hanging around some guys who were going to drive through the South, dropping off flyers and posters advertising the festival from New Orleans to Atlanta.

They were then heading up to Woodstock, which was the first of the three venues to host this traveling pop festival. (Dallas and New Orleans were going to take place on Labor Day weekend, with the artists flying back and forth to each.) I went along for the ride, more in hopes of sleeping with her than anything else. I had $40 in my pocket, half of which was spent on a sleeping bag. But I wasn't concerned: money went further back then.

We smoked pot and took white capsules of mescaline the whole way, and got to Woodstock three days early. There weren't many people there yet, so we set up camp in a deserted field that had a few scattered tents breaking the landscape and then wandered around to the area where they were building the stage.

Before long, I noticed a tall, mutton chopped man who called himself Chip Monck shouting orders. Within hours, he would become the voice of Woodstock, but at that point, he was just a nice guy with a lot to do. He agreed to let me work for him on stage but on the condition that I was to "stay out of everyone's way and out of sight." He then put me in charge of adjusting a cable on the main stage so it stayed where it was supposed to be, so that no one would trip over it.

(What he didn't tell me - or anyone else - was that they were making a movie about the festival. It wasn't until the movie came out that I realized that I had been working for the cameraman. I've watched every frame of it since then multiple times, and am proud to say you can't see me, except perhaps for a second during "The Star Spangled Banner." And even then I'm not sure it's me.)

By the time we got settled, people had started to pile into the festival grounds. Before the night was done, stagehands were estimating that 30,000 people were already camped out. Since only about 30,000 tickets had been sold, it was the first indication that something big was afoot.

As the crowd grew, we graduated from mescaline to acid, and stuck with it throughout the festival. This was the LSD you drank, often from one of those bladder-shaped wineskins that you passed around from hand to hand. It was a mellow kind of high, and lasted so long that we started referring to it not as a trip, but a tour.

By today's standards, the stage, if not the entire event, was primitive. The backstage pass was made out of cardboard and hand-written. You kept it in your pocket, and pulled it out whenever you had to get back on the stage. And backstage was just that -- the back of the stage.

I spent the entire festival on the main stage, watching my cable and mixing with everyone. While it's difficult now not to think of Woodstock in terms of clichés, there was a special camaraderie there that I don't think had ever happened before or, for that matter, since.
That was why, despite all the difficulties and discomfort, no one complained. We were always able to ferry the artists in and out of the festival, but most of them stayed there, taking swigs from the wine skins, waiting to see what would happen next.

The unpredictability was part of the fun. We were running hopelessly behind schedule from the outset, but that often had spectacular results. Jimi Hendrix, for instance, was scheduled to go on at 11 P.M., but didn't get on until five in the morning, which set the stage for his perfectly timed rendition of "The Star Spangled Banner" at sunrise. Had we been on time, it probably wouldn't have been the same.

By Woodstock's end, I knew my life had been changed forever. I had hung out with people like Richie Havens and Alvin Lee of Ten Years After (in whose honor I bought a pair of white clogs), and had seen things well beyond the reach of my 19-year-old imagination.

On the long drive south, I couldn't stop thinking about the week. I had never worked so hard in my life, and had never had as much fun. This was sort of a big deal because my father, who wanted to instill a good work ethic in me, had encouraged me to get afterschool and summer jobs. And even though I had never been afraid of work, school and the jobs I had suffered through had been drudgery.

This had been anything but. This had been fun. Even though I worked 14 hours a day pulling a cable, I felt so much a part of what was happening that I wanted it to last forever. It was like that cable had been my umbilical cord, and when I unplugged it, my life, for real, had begun.

That feeling lasted about as long as the drive home. Because I had lied to my parents, who thought I was visiting a friend in Texas, no one knew where I had been. So although I couldn't stop thinking about Woodstock, I couldn't talk about it to anyone.

So, while my mind was still in Woodstock, my body was trapped in New Orleans, robotically getting ready for college. Woodstock seemed as far away as Mars.

My attitude didn't get better once school started, so it's no great surprise that I spent freshman year partying, getting miserable grades, and convincing myself I would never fit in. If for that reason alone, finding out that a friend's older brother was coming back from Chicago with some shady investors and opening up a Fillmore of the South was the best news I had heard in a long time.

As a point of context, up until Woodstock, most cities didn't have a club like the Fillmore for rock bands to play. Traditionally, the concert business was dominated by radio shows and record labels, who would package a lengthy lineup of groups or singers with a hit single. The band would sing three songs and get off the stage.

Then artists like the Beatles, the Rolling Stones, and Bob Dylan made albums complete song cycles and prompted the growth of AOR FM (album-oriented radio). Now, most rock groups had full sets of material at their disposal and wanted longer stage sets to showcase the work.

Woodstock, both the festival and the movie, was proof of concept, documenting how different young audience expectations for live music had become. None of this was lost on the great promoters, like the grand impresario, Bill Graham, who was to become a hero and mentor to me. He quickly grasped the potential of the concert industry and, in no short order, opened two clubs, The Fillmore (in San Francisco) and The Fillmore East (in New York), that would come to define an era.

In 1969, following Graham's lead, a group out of Chicago, headed by Bill Johnston, a native New Orleanian, wanted to set up a hall in their hometown. He ran a successful counter-culture bar called Barnaby's, where Chicago Transit Authority, before the name change to just Chicago (Mayor Daley successfully sued the band to change the name), was the house band. A number of Bill's friends were involved in a bar called Your Father's Moustache, so the owners, thinking it would be funny, petitioned to change the club's name to Your Mother's Beaver.

This against the backdrop of a town reeling from the effects of the 1968 Democratic Convention riots. Despite public outrage, the Daley administration had hardened its position on the counter culture, turned down the request, and essentially ran the group out of town.

Johnston knew the basic idea -- finding an old warehouse or gym, putting a stage into it, and using the open area for festival seating (no chairs, no reserved seats) -- could work as well in any number of cities as it did in San Francisco and New York. But New Orleans was home, and where he wanted to be. So, in 1969, he came back home, and because of that, suddenly, I had a plan.

The Seventies:
Leave It to Beaver's

As soon as the Beavers came to town, they hired my friend Jay, who was Bill Johnston's younger brother, to find a venue. With Woodstock still fresh in my mind, I hung around Jay until I managed to get myself hired.

Somehow, between Jay, Bill and the real estate agents, they came up with a 150-year-old cotton warehouse in the worst part of town. First we had to convert the building, which had been built around 1803, into a concert hall. We cleaned it up, built a large stage, a small office, dressing rooms, bleachers, and concession stands, and left a large open area in front of the stage. By the time we were done, it had become The Warehouse. We could sell 1,800 tickets before hitting legal capacity; although, we'd later cram more than 5,000 people into the room.

Even from the beginning, we knew we had opened a club that rock bands couldn't wait to play. The opening show was scheduled for two nights, Friday January 30th and Saturday January 31st, and included the Grateful Dead, the original Fleetwood Mac, and The Flock (a band out of Chicago who, although now forgotten, had a big buzz).

We sold maybe 500 tickets the first night ($3.50 in advance, four bucks at the door) and about 750 the second. The shows went off without a hitch, but around midnight on the last night, after the concert was over, the FBI and the local police arrived, like something out of *Dragnet*.

The police had been used to bar hours, so they had timed their arrival to when they expected things to just be heating up. But the show had, in fact, been over for hours.

So the policemen didn't know what to think when Jay, who doubled as the night watchman, was sleeping there, opened the door in his underwear and told the policeman there was no one inside but a few of his security staff.

Wanting bigger fish than a bunch of scraggly hippies, the police barrelled down to the hotel where the group was staying and promptly busted everyone there, including Jerry Garcia, whose head split open when they kicked in the door of his hotel room.

They did manage to find a little pot in Garcia's room. While hardly the big prize they had been chasing, it was enough to get the band arrested.

Even so, with Jerry in chains, they turned their full attention towards one Stanley Owsley. Owsley was a chemist, the Dead's lighting and sound engineer, and, most importantly, the maker of the best LSD in the country.

A veteran not just of the Dead's entourage, he had also been one of the Merry Pranksters, a legendary traveling drug and counterculture circus that had, among other things, dedicated itself to introducing LSD to America. As a result, in certain circles, he was far more infamous than the musicians and writers who surrounded him.

One of the great things about Owsley was his ability to get along with anyone. His charm even worked on our 40-year-old electrician, a "straight" named Stanley Chotin, who had never introduced anything stronger than a beer into his system.

The two had unexpectedly hit it off after bonding over some wiring problem. Somewhere along the line, not knowing that the wine was laced with acid, Stanley had taken a few swigs from the wineskin. Which helped explain why the two disappeared right after the concert - for three days.

The incident ended happily for all. The Stanleys eluded the police and, inspired by the events of that night, the Dead ended up with their most famous song, "Trucking," and the pivotal lyric, "Busted down on Bourbon street, set up like a bowling pin/knocked down, it gets to wearing thin, they just won't let you be, oh no."

Not bad, I'd say, for a venue's first weekend.

The Smoke Patrol

In the course of my time at the Warehouse, I'd end up doing many things, but I got my first real foot in the door as its head of security. It was not the kind of job well-to-do kids from good, professional families in New Orleans would typically go after, but it seemed like a perfect fit to me.

I was lucky in that my father was a doctor, and my mother was loving. I had three sisters, and we all lived in a very nice house in uptown New Orleans. But I was a short and sickly kid and wanted nothing more than to be an athlete, spending days playing baseball and football with the neighborhood kids.

My mother, who was born and raised in Australia, thought that American sports were brutal and steered me into swimming instead. It turned out that I was good at it and had the discipline involved with being a competitive swimmer. I'd go to a swimming practice before school, after school, and in the evening. My dream was to get to the Olympic tryouts, and I pushed myself until I had earned a reputation throughout the south.

Then I came up against a problem I couldn't fix. While everyone else started to grow, I stayed short. That cut my national swimming career off at, so to speak, the knees. I continued to train and managed to win a high school state championship, but I knew that was as far as a guy my size was going to get.

I also realized that while I wasn't going to get taller, I

could always get stronger. It wasn't a new idea - I'd been fascinated by muscles since the *Tarzan* movies. Sitting on my dad's lap watching them, I envisioned myself swinging through trees, fighting the alligators, and beating up the bad guys. Then, in 1958, I saw the first *Hercules* movie, and I knew that was who I wanted to be.

As you'd expect from a kid who loved Tarzan and Hercules, I was also totally into superhero comic books. Each of them ran ads for Charles Atlas, ads that promised Charles would turn you into a real man.

The message was not lost on me. Night after night, for the next four years, I'd beg my father for a chance to buy those weights. But he'd explain that he didn't want me lifting weights until my bones were strong enough to handle the strain.

Finally, when I turned 12, he gave in and let me get a Charles Atlas weight set. I still remember how it felt when I got to lift those plastic, sand-filled barbell sets out of the box.

Charles Atlas more than lived up to his promise. Those weights rescued me from becoming the small kid who got sand kicked in his face by the neighborhood bullies. Those weights made me feel like a man.

As I got stronger, my grandfather, who had been a boxer, convinced me to add boxing to my training. I enjoyed it and even boxed in Golden Gloves for several years, but I didn't want to get the beat-up look most boxers end up with. But I didn't lose the attitude, so most of my fights ended up out of the ring.

This tough guy bravado kept me in constant trouble at school. After a slew of suspensions, my parents threw up their hands and sent me to Saint Paul's High School, a boarding school 75 miles from New Orleans.

The school was run by the Christian Brothers, an order of Catholic men who knew a thing or two about discipline. My parents felt that the 24-hour supervision would help me turn a new leaf.

It did, but not in the way they had hoped. Because the first and most important lesson I learned there was how to talk my way out of anything.

The rule there was that if you stayed out of trouble, you only had to spend one weekend a month at the school. Most of us were from New Orleans, and no one wanted to stay there on the weekend. So, although I was far from a model student, I cultivated a golden tongue and managed to leave every single weekend in the two years I was there. (Even better, my parents thought I was at school and never knew where I was on any given weekend.)

The second great thing about the school was its little gym, which I could use anytime I wanted to. At the time, most coaches thought that weight training undermined agility, so at first I had the gym to myself. Then Don Joyce, the young son of an all-pro football player, who was a foot taller and at 230 pounds, substantially stronger than me, started working out too. He knew more than I did about it and taught me how to incorporate three different power lifts (the bench press, the squat and the deadlift) into a workout.

At the time, I wanted to be a bodybuilder like my idol, Steve Reeves. Once again, though, my height worked against me, because short guys that get too big look less like a hero than a stuffed sausage, bursting at the seams. So while I still almost set national records in squats, bench presses, and deadlifts, I knew I could only go so far as a bodybuilder.

That didn't stop me from being a muscular fireplug and an asshole, which both proved to be excellent qualifications for a job working security at the Warehouse. We hired a number of ex-athletes and football players to round out the squad. One of them owned a gym, so me and the other guys would train there. Before too long, we even had a name: the Smoke Patrol.

We got the name because we were constantly on the lookout for anyone smoking a cigarette inside the building. It had nothing to do with health regulations -- people still smoked in doctor's offices and restaurants and airplanes back then. And realistically, there was little chance that a cigarette would have torched the building.

Instead, it was because the city, looking for an excuse to shut us down, had seized on an obscure, widely ignored sanction against smoking and threatened to pull the plug the minute they saw someone with a lit cigarette. They seemed to be serious, so, with the Warehouse's survival at stake, we enforced the ban with a vengeance.

On top of that, there always seemed to be a lot of pent up violence inside the club. On average, we'd deal with five fights a night. All of them seemed to happen right in front of me at one set of bleachers. I couldn't understand what it was about those bleachers. Then a girl set me straight, and changed my world.

The whole thing started when my friend, David Doyle, tried to pick up a girl he saw in the stands. Afraid to go out with him by herself, she told him she'd go, but only if he found a date for her friend. David asked me to help him out and pointed the girl out.

Her name was Penny, and she was a cute, full-figured brunette. I actually was more interested in his date, but rather than rock the boat, we went to the Red Lion, a popular local bar.

In the course of the evening, I asked Penny why she thought all the fights broke out in front of that one bleacher. She explained that all the kids from the west bank of town sat on that bleacher because it was on the west side of the club.

Compared to those of us from the east side, the West Bank was a rowdier, "other side of the tracks" bunch. They hated me and had nicknamed me The Little General, because they thought I was busting people for smoking pot. Or just busting people.

I knew about the name -- it had been given to me by the underground press -- but I was really surprised how people used it. I thought the nickname was a tribute to my prowess, and that it was a sign of respect.

It never occurred to me that most of the young people in New Orleans just thought I was a jerk and a bully.

By way of a peace offering, I explained what was at stake with the smoking ban. Then I showed her where the kids could smoke pot without getting caught, and asked her to pass the information along to the rest of her friends. She wasted no time in doing so. From that day on, I had a lot less trouble.

That night, while we were talking, a girl I knew walked into the bar. David took one look at her, lost all interest in his date, and had me introduce them to each other. They got married two years later, and Penny and I got married two years after that. You have to wonder, what are the odds of two friends introducing each other to their prospective wives at the same bar on the same night?

Signs of Life

I was good at security, but before too long, I knew I really wanted to run production. In 1973, when I was just 23, The Warehouse had fallen on some financial hard times. My father gave them some money to get them through, which gave me the leverage I needed to become a partner in the business. I was the youngest and the greenest, but everyone else wanted out of production, so the job was mine.

I got my first real taste of my new life on a tour of southern colleges with one of my heroes, Jerry Jeff Walker, who was fronting the legendary Texas group, The Lost Gonzo Band. The opening act? A guy named

Jimmy Buffett and the Coral Reefers, who had just scored their first hit.

The tour itself runs together in my mind even more than most, because the bands were interchangeable. Sometimes the Coral Reefers played with Jerry Jeff Walker and the Lost Gonzo Band for Jimmy Buffett, and sometimes they played it straight. You never knew what was going to happen. All you knew was that it was bound to be good.

Even at the best of those shows, though, the music really didn't get started until later on. Every night, after the show was over, they would go back to the hotel, play bluegrass, and pick until dawn. I don't think anything ever felt as real as those nights.

Doors of Perception

No matter how much fun I would have on the road, the Warehouse was my home. Everyone played there except The Beatles and the Rolling Stones. The Who did the last performance of *Tommy* there, as well as Jim Morrison, who did his last concert at the Warehouse.

By the time they finally made it to New Orleans, the Doors were the biggest, most exciting band in the world. I had been a big fan and was determined to treat them right.

To me, that meant meeting them at the airport, which, back then, was a relatively new development. Up until around 1970 or so, bands didn't expect special treatment and would generally take care of themselves.

Then, all of a sudden, everyone started attaching riders to their contracts, specifying food, chauffeurs, etc. Because the subsequent limo bills were killing us, we bought two limousines from a mortuary in Lake Charles. And I made sure both of them were at the airport waiting.

By the time the band walked out of the airport, the tension between them could not be more obvious. Without saying a word, Morrison got in one limo and the rest of the band got in the other. I quickly decided to go with Jim, by far the most charismatic, and climbed in the back seat with him. Without any preliminaries, he asked me if I had any drugs.

I told him that I could get him anything he wanted, but wasn't holding anything at the moment. As if by design, the limo driver chimed in saying, "I have some raw opium." A quick conversation revealed that neither Morrison nor I had ever done raw opium before. Rather than let the lack of expertise deter us, we sat in the back, eating it without thinking to ask how much we should take and what effect it would have on us.

For most of the gig, Morrison looked none the worse for wear. Until "Light My Fire," during which Morrison, who was wobbling from the opium, lost his balance, fell back into the drum kit, and didn't get up. The band looked at him for a minute and then left the stage.

The audience was frozen by the moment. Unclear

whether this was part of the show or not, they stood there without moving. Finally, someone yelled, "show us your dick, Jim."

But Jim remained on the ground in a fetal position. Then, without moving, he started singing again, picking up exactly where the song had stopped. The band heard him singing, came back on stage, and finished the song and the set. Morrison went to Paris soon after, and died several weeks later. The Warehouse was the last stage he ever played on.

Careful with that Axe, Eugene

Pink Floyd had become big fans of the Warehouse, and we always looked forward to their dates. But they always had a surprise up their sleeve.

Their first time at The Warehouse, we were flabbergasted when a 24-foot truck showed up carrying lighting gear. Up until then, everyone had used our shitty lighting system, but Pink Floyd wanted their own. Next time around, now at arenas, they showed up with their own sound system, another first, and then with their own stage.

That first time, we had loaded all the equipment back into the truck after the show and gone back inside and taken acid. At some point during the night, someone noticed that the truck had vanished. Our police called the city police, and put out an APB on it.

By doing so, it became, by definition, an interstate crime and, thus, was under FBI jurisdiction. As a person involved in production, I was one of the people the agents had to talk to. Even if I, like most of the people in the room, was still tripping.

Luckily, the agents decided to take a roadie out and search for the truck, which was quickly found undamaged on the side of a road in Gentilly, a neighborhood east of New Orleans. It was pretty apparent that someone had just taken the truck for a joyride, completely oblivious to the contents inside it.

Elvis is in the Building

Because rock was still making up the rules as it went along, celebrities were far more accessible then than they are now. So without doing anything really to deserve it, you'd find yourself in a conversation with legends who automatically tossed out lessons that you'd remember for years.

The only time I ever worked with Elvis, for instance, was on a few dates in 1974, that Beaver Productions was promoting. By that time, I was used to handling the production of shows outside New Orleans. In this instance, we were in Mobile, Alabama.

For no apparent reason, Colonel Tom Parker, Elvis's larger-than-life manager, took a liking to me.

Parker told me all kinds of stories about the music business. He then said that I should get out of concert promotion and into artist management work, because promoters had to steal for a living. Promoters were so bad, he said, that he spent most of his time at the shows finding out how the promoters were cheating him.

Especially in light of what was to come out later about his dealings with Elvis, I should have said what I was thinking, that promoters' margins were so small that they had to make money where they could. The reason that the margins were so small was simply because of people like him.

I wasn't kidding. To put on a concert, promoters factored in the artist's guaranteed fee and their own small profit, and then went about the business of promoting and producing the concert. After the expenses from the production were deducted from the revenue, the promoters and the artist split the figure.

In the beginning, the traditional split was 60/40% in favor of the artist. But in 1971, with the advent of Concerts West, the first national promoters' firm, the split went up to 90/10%. If that wasn't bad enough, promoters incurred all the expenses and took all the risk, and that one bad show could wipe out a streak of successful ones.

The only way a promoter could shift his odds a hair was by padding expenses. So Parker in his own way was right -- promoters were in fact cheating. But it seemed to me more a matter of survival than of greed.

Fortunately, I held my tongue. He told me if I ever wanted a job, I should give him a call. Then he took me backstage to meet the King.

Although, I had been working in the field for five years and had gotten used to meeting rock stars by then, Elvis was another thing entirely. He was wearing one of the rhinestone jumpsuits and, fully inhabiting the total Vegas look he had developed, was almost a caricature of himself.

Despite that, I was as nervous as he was bloated about meeting him. He seemed distracted and out of it, but he still gave me his trademark smile. I told him how awesome it was to meet him, to which he replied, "thank you, thank you very much."

Admittedly, it wasn't a lot to base a relationship on, but it didn't matter. I had met the King.

The Fall and Rise of Ziggy Stardust

While Elvis' golden years were winding down, I was equally excited to meet David Bowie. He was still relatively unknown and going through a gay phase. His booking agent called us and said David had wanted to play the Warehouse, largely to tap into New Orleans' gay community.

We told him that we didn't think he'd sell 50 tickets, but the agent was insistent. Since his booking agency handled most of the artists we featured, we gave in, taking the 90/10% deal. In the end, 600 to 700 people came, and probably half of them were on the guest list.

Even though the show didn't come close to selling out, there was no doubt in anyone's mind that Bowie was going to be a major star. So we were surprised when

Bowie himself, rather than one of his "people," came into our office to settle up.

"Great to see you," Don Fox told him. "You owe us three grand."

Now, when Don Fox talks, people listen. He had come down from Chicago in 1970 to manage the club, and had quickly replaced one of the early partners. Fox was -- and is -- a man's man, and was my direct boss. A big, mean guy and a true fighter, he immediately commanded respect from even the most rowdy bands and crew.

Bowie was no exception. Still, he never expected to be stuck with a $3,000 bill. "What do you mean?" he said.

Fox showed him all the expenses, explained the deal, and then, with a big flourish, shrugged it off and tore up the invoice, telling Bowie not to worry. He had been kidding the whole time, but had succeeded in giving the man who fell to earth a real scare.

Eat a Peach

It hadn't taken me long to grow into my expanded role in production or become comfortable with venues of all sizes, but every once in awhile, you had to be especially fast on your feet. A July 4, 1974 concert featuring the Allman Brothers and ZZ Top at the Mobile Senior Bowl, which held 70,000 people, was one of those times.

The night before the show, Dickie Betts and Greg Allman had gotten into a fight at the Holiday Inn around two in the morning, and gotten arrested. We went down to the police department, which was as redneck as it got, and were told by the sheriff that we were "shit out of luck."

Clearly enjoying himself, the sheriff went on to explain that the judge was away on a holiday vacation, so the two rockers were going to be in jail until Monday. "You've got a problem," he said, barely keeping the smirk off his face.

"No," I said, looking straight at him. "We don't have a problem. You have a problem."

I pointed out that with 60,000 to 70,000 people heading into the city to see the Allman Brothers, he was facing a potential riot. Then, in a visible demonstration of his influence, Buddy Clewis, an old colleague who managed all the public facilities in Mobile and wielded tremendous influence, got the judge to tell them to drop the charges and let the concert go on.

The next night, the police and fire department were out in full force, almost willing something to go wrong and give them an excuse to step in. After a few opening acts, ZZ Top went on stage.

In the middle of their set, someone in the audience started shooting fireworks. One landed on the stage's canvas roof, which started to smolder. The fire department chief grabbed me and ordered me to go out and tell people to stop with the fireworks or they would pull the plug then and there.

Not knowing what else to do, I grabbed an open mike, interrupted Billy Gibbons between songs, and explained that the fire marshal was going to shut the show down if the fireworks didn't stop. I had barely finished when ZZ Top's manager, Bill Ham, walked up to me screaming that no one was allowed to go on stage while the band was playing and threw a punch at me. He never let me explain and never accepted me after that.

That hurt because I not only loved ZZ Top but had helped get them their first New Orleans gig early on. I was friends with Billy's younger sister, who had told him all about the Warehouse. They were so excited that they drove in from Texas on a night that Quicksilver Messenger Service, The Allman Brothers, and a now forgotten horn band called Chase were playing.

Billy asked me how they could get on the bill. The answer was that they couldn't. But they were so enthusiastic that I finally went over to Don Fox, explained the situation, and got Fox to talk to them.

Somehow, they managed to talk Fox into letting them play a 20-minute set, which was no easy feat. Their short performance ended up blowing people away, and giving Chase an impossible act to follow.

The night's surprises didn't end there. The Allmans, who were local heroes, were used to playing for two to three hours at a time. But they weren't the headliners, so Fox had to tell them they were only allowed to play for 45 minutes. They weren't happy about it, but kept their set to just under an hour.

Quicksilver followed with their standard 60-minute plus encore set. They said goodnight and left via the catwalk that went from the stage to the dressing room. This was a narrow passage, so they weren't expecting the Allmans heading towards them, instruments in tow. Walking past the headliners, without any announcement or fanfare, the Allman Brothers retook the stage and played for another two or three hours.

Not incidentally, from that night on, Fox became Z.Z. Top's promoter. One of their songs had been getting airplay in Boston, so they wanted to go up there and play. As promoters, it put us in a funny position. First, we weren't going to be able to make any money off the gig. And second, we didn't like it when out-of-town promoters poached our shows, and didn't want to intrude on the local promoters' turf.

To get around that, we worked with a local radio station and set up a free concert in the Boston Commons. We hoped a few thousand people would show, but we ended up with over 30,000 fans.

The band was ecstatic, but the radio station, which got stuck with $50,000 in damages from the city, was less so. It put the band on the map in the northeast, but it also resulted in a ban on free concerts in the Boston Commons that lingered on for decades.

The Boss and the Road Not Taken

Fox and Johnston were a very successful team, but by

1975, it was obvious that they couldn't work together anymore. Everyone knew one of them would have to leave, and I was torn between Bill Johnston, my original mentor, and Don Fox, who was a terrific promoter but not the mentor Bill was.

Even though he started the company, Bill, who was tired of the concert business, refused to fight and left the company, ostensibly to pursue new opportunities in artist management. Remembering my conversation with Colonel Parker, I decided to cast my fate with Bill.

Until we could find some musicians to manage, we started another concert promotion company called Roadside Attractions and booked concerts with unknown artists such as Gino Vannelli, a Canadian singer from Montreal, and Bruce Springsteen, a folk singer from New Jersey.

I had been a Springsteen fan for a couple of years, solely on the strength of his first two records. Even though the albums had not sold well, I loved them and was convinced Springsteen was the next great rock star. Bill was a master promoter, so I got him to work with the local radio stations and drum up awareness for this emerging phenomenon. As a result, New Orleans was the first place outside of the New Jersey area that Springsteen broke out in.

That changed quickly. In 1975, Springsteen released *Born To Run* and was heralded on the covers of both *Newsweek* and *Time,* who never agreed on anything, as the new face of Rock & Roll.

I was already convinced, but I couldn't make Bill

understand. Nor was I alone -- Michael Pillot, a friend from New Orleans and later my partner in my first music video company, was a rising executive at Columbia Records and responsible for Bruce at the label. He also tried to get Bill interested, but he too hit a dead end.

Johnston was still in the process of negotiating a management deal with Gino Vannelli when, in the middle of the night, Bruce called to say he had just fired his manager, Mike Appel, and wanted Bill to manage him. To my amazement, Bill turned him down -- for Gino Vannelli! I can only imagine how different my life would have been, had only he listened.

Under the Dome

Around the same time, we missed yet another big opportunity. One of our new partners had gotten involved with Pace Productions, a sports production company specializing in motocross and other sports related events.

Run by Alan Becker and financed by old Houston money, in 1975, Pace had secured the grand opening of what New Orleans was calling the eighth wonder of the world, the Super Dome. It was scheduled to open over the Labor Day weekend and was going to feature three days of entertainment, culminating in the Saints' season opener.

Not being in the concert business, Pace hired a New York promoter named Ron Delsener to book the talent. At the time, concert promotion was extremely territorial; "poaching" other promoters' markets was considered bad form. But Ron Delsener, who was and remains the personification of a promoter, didn't see it that way and thought he could fly down and steal our market.

Closing ranks against the Yankee carpetbagger, the local community enlisted the help of an allegedly corrupt New Orleans lawyer/politician (not so unusual in New Orleans). He threatened to have Delsener arrested on charges of cocaine distribution if he didn't leave the city within 48 hours. The threat worked, and by default we became the concert bookers for the grand opening of the Superdome.

Our first show was for the adults and starred Bob Hope and a number of big bands from the 1940s and 1950s. Next was a soul show featuring Motown recording acts, and the third was a Southern Rock showcase, featuring The Allman Brothers, The Marshall Tucker Band, Wet Willie and Lynyrd Skynyrd.

The shows went off smoothly, and, flush with success, Pace decided they'd become a real concert promotion company and asked us to run it. It was as good an opportunity as it gets, but Bill, who had decided to move to California, wasn't interested.

I couldn't see myself staying in the concert business or moving by myself to Houston, so I told Bill I'd move out with him. I can't say we were missed. Under the direction of our partner, Louie Messina, Pace first morphed into the entertainment giant, SFX, then Clear Channel and, finally, Live Nation.

This is the Story of Hurricane

While getting ready to move to California, I got involved with a guy called "Hurricane Clyde," who was putting together a big benefit in New Orleans for former boxer and convicted murderer, Rueben Hurricane Carter. His goal? To raise awareness about Carter and get him pardoned.

I knew that New Orleans would balk at the politics behind the event, so we convinced him to move the show to Houston Astrodome, which proved far more hospitable.

The performance was slated for January 26, 1976. Led by Bob Dylan, it quickly became a who's who of big stars, including artists such as Stevie Wonder and Isaac Hayes, all of whom played for expenses. More than 41,000 people paid $12.50 each to get in, but, as I was to learn, as in most of these concerts, very little money actually went to the cause. And I learned that lesson from none other than Bill Graham, one of my biggest heroes, himself.

As the person running the production of the show, I got to hire his company to do all the stage lighting and sound production. When I finally got to meet him, I started to complain about how much money he was charging for a show that was a benefit. He patiently listened to me go on and on about how it was for a charity and a good cause. After I had finished vomiting my idealism, he simply said, "When I give to a charity, I write a check. When I work for a charity, they write the check."

Then, in a comment that was later verified by *Rolling Stone* magazine, he showed me how most charity concerts were far less about the cause and far more about rock stars treating themselves lavishly under the belief that they were doing a good thing. The cause, he explained, was an afterthought, if that.

Rolling Stone agreed, running two stories on the show's finances. On March 24, 1977, respected journalist Chet Flippo reported that of the $600,000 raised in Houston and in a sister concert in Madison Square Garden, only $100,000 made its way to the legal defense fund.

As if to rub salt in the wound, I went to Rahway State Prison and met with Carter, who was later to be played by Denzel Washington in a whitewashed biopic. I remember looking into his eyes and seeing a vicious killer. He may or may not have been guilty of this particular murder, I thought as I walked out of the prison, but he had definitely killed someone else.

That job cost me my idealistic maidenhood. At least the timing on it was right, because as soon as it ended, I was on my way to Los Angeles, a place where it wouldn't be missed.

Disco Inferno

Penny and I had married in 1974, but I moved to Los Angeles by myself in late 1975 to get things started out there. While Bill was figuring the company out, I went to work with Lewis Grey, the nationwide promoter of most of the big black acts, such as the Ohio Players, the Bar-Kays, George Clinton and P. Funk, Lionel Richie and the Commodores, Earth, Wind, and Fire, and Tower of Power.

Lewis was not just an incredible promoter who knew his markets and his artists, but he was also an absolutely lovely man who taught me about the day-to-day workings of the music industry.

Although black music typically had been confined to clubs and small venues, we brought them into outdoor dates and arenas. The only problem was that the festival shows were often marred by violent riots. At Kansas City's Arrowhead Stadium, for instance, a man fired a handgun into the audience, inciting a panic among the 75,000 people in the stadium.

The aftermath of the show was horrific. I remember moving through the area in front of the stage, thinking it looked like a battle had taken place. Bloodied clothes were everywhere. I used to tell people that we found shoes with feet still in them, which was an exaggeration for sure, but an image that didn't seem too far off the mark.

There had also been trouble at a Houston stadium and the Los Angeles Coliseum, so I could only imagine the trouble we were about to have with a New Year's Eve extravaganza scheduled for the Superdome. It featured, among others, Earth, Wind, and Fire, and was taking place the night before the Georgia Bulldogs were to play Tony Dorsett's Pittsburgh's team for the national championship.

New Orleans was still a closed, racist society, and the white power elite were not happy with the idea of 60,000 black people gathering on New Year's Eve in New Orleans, in front of the national media, who had flocked to town for the game.

In a closed door meeting, the city came up with every possible excuse to cancel the event, but I kept coming up with solutions to all their problems. Finally, out of reasons and patience, they abandoned the charade and just told us they were shutting us down.

We had already spent a lot of time and money on a show that was now just a few days away. Since I came from an old New Orleans family, they agreed to a post-cancellation meeting in which, as the ritual went, I would plead -- unsuccessfully -- that the show must go on.

And so it was that I entered a large boardroom at the exclusive, all-white Petroleum Club, in front of some of New Orleans' most powerful and haughty businessmen. I walked in with Lewis Grey, the producer of the event, and several black attorneys. I was greeted with indulgent smiles from men I had grown up with all my life. We then went through the excuses once again. They reiterated that the concert didn't give them enough time to prepare for the game. We reminded them that we had already done exactly that during the Dome's opening.

Facts did nothing to stop their continued nitpicking or the racism that was obviously behind their objections. Rather than freak out, I simply told them that a white show would have been rubber stamped. But as they had shown with Hurricane Carter, the New Orleans elite did not want black shows at the Superdome.

Before they could even begin to protest, I informed them that we had contacted the NAACP and the black members of both football teams, including Tony Dorsett (pure bluff, that) and that there would be a boycott of the Sugar Bowl if the concert did not go on as planned.

Although I hadn't talked to the players, I had no doubt that they would be behind the boycott. I must have been convincing enough to frighten the fat cats, who reinstated the concert.

As a point of personal pride, I'm happy to report that the show went off without a hitch. It seemed like a perfect way to break all ties with New Orleans and make a fresh start in Malibu.

**The Eighties:
Ready for My Close Up**

After close to two years working with Lewis Grey, Bill solidified the deal with Gino Vannelli, and, in 1978, my principal job became running Gino's production and tour. I enjoyed going on the road, and not just because of the music. Most of the facilities we played were sports arenas that had gyms, so I didn't have to give up my training for the road.

But the tour and the management company were slowly falling apart. Towards the end of the tour, in early 1979, Gino and Bill split up, leaving me without mentors or a clear direction for the first time in years.

Kevin Wall, who I had met at the Earth, Wind, and Fire concert, and I decided to try our hands at the roller skating fad that had captured the country's imagination, making and importing multi-colored boots from Taiwan. We got a surf/skate company to assemble the wheels, and we sold the skates. We made a little bit of money, but it was a giant headache and an obvious dead end.

To make it worse, despite our personal problems, in 1979 Penny was pregnant, which put the pressure on me to find work. Tired of the rock and roll circus, I called my sister Ann, who was an actress living in New York and was married to Mal Mellon. Mal was an executive producer for a top commercial production company, Levine/Pitka Productions.

In my years at the Warehouse, I had been around crews shooting concert films of performers such as Leon Russell and Wings and believed it to be a developing medium. In what seemed like a natural progression, I decided to shift my focus from concert to film production.

So we moved to New York, and I went to work for my brother-in-law as a $40 a day PA. It was quite a comedown from being a highly paid production manager, but I quickly learned the medium and six months later had become an in-demand commercial producer specializing in difficult jobs in far-off locations.

During that time, March 1980, my first child, Abigail, was born and my second, a boy, Holland, was conceived in late 1981. I loved my daughter and knew I'd love my son, but the marriage itself was intolerable. We had both checked out of it and were holding on out of sheer tenacity.

Work, in the meantime, was a whirlwind and a great escape. I had skyrocketed up the production ladder and was flying all over the world. Greg Ramsey, a commercial producer who'd given me a start as a production assistant, wanted to become a director and, somehow, had been contacted by an up and coming English band, A Flock of Seagulls.

They wanted him to direct a "promo" for the band's new single. Because of my background in music, Greg asked me to produce it. We shot the performance-based video on his rooftop in New York.

From that, later in 1981, Journey's management asked me to consult on a shoot of one of their shows. Since they were the only people doing multi-camera work at the time, we hired NFL Films to shoot it. Not surprisingly, the concert ended up looking like a sporting event. To do this right, I realized, we'd have to develop crews who had a feel for music.

Sensing an opportunity, I started my first music video company, Cinerock, under the wings of a commercial production company, Philip Landeck Productions, several months later. I used the commercial, boutique company approach, and Michael Pillot joined with me as Executive Producer (salesman).

One of the great unsung consequences of these early music videos was its role in shattering the glass ceiling of the "good ole' boy" network that ruled the music industry. Up until then, there were many women working at the labels, but none held executive positions at any of the major labels. Instead, they were usually "executive assistants," a.k.a secretaries.

Since few of the men wanted to have anything to do with music video, it was a logical opportunity for women like Debbie Newman, who had worked at Columbia Records for years, to move up the ladder. Because she was the first, I nicknamed these women "The Debbies." She, Liz Heller at MCA, and Randy Skinner at Warner Brothers, among others, came to dominate the music video industry and kept me busy shooting song-based shorts for what were then called "promos."

Even so, none of us were prepared for MTV. The first time I turned it on I saw two of our videos -- a Journey song and a Flock of Seagulls video -- air within the first few hours. Suddenly, like the music video field itself, Cinerock was up and running.

I Want My MTV

As with my days at the Warehouse, this was clearly a place of being in the right place at the right time. Within a few years, companies I owned or was a major part of had produced a ton of videos. Sensing the benefit of an in-house production team, Capitol Records bought Cinerock, which turned into Picture Music.

I ran the New York operation from wonderful offices at the foot of Madison Avenue, producing videos for artists such as Journey, Billy Idol, Elton John, Jazzy Jeff and the Fresh Prince, Yes, Tom Petty and the Heartbreakers, Cyndi Lauper, Michael Jackson, New Kids on the Block, Queen Latifah, Marky Mark, and many, many others. It was an incredibly exciting time, fueled by drugs, spontaneity, creativity, and adrenaline.

There was a feeling in those days that anything could happen and could happen quickly. I was at the famous New York City nightclub Limelight, for instance, when the video for "White Wedding" by Billy Idol came on. As soon as I saw him, I knew that I wanted to work with him.

It proved as easy as a phone call to his manager, Bill Aucoin, who I had already done business with. He set up a meeting while Billy was on tour supporting the *Rebel Yell* album. I went up to Vermont and hit it off immediately.

From the outset, I thought he and his cheekbones could transform punk into punk chic. I told him that he should always be photographed like a high fashion model and wanted Tony Mitchell, my favorite commercial Director of Photography, as well as Jeff Stein and the rest of the team, to do it first.

We shot "Rebel Yell," the song that launched his solo career, in 16 mm, but Jeff, who was deaf to anyone else's input, turned in a video that was just okay. So rather than make the same mistake twice, I hired David

Mallet, already a respected veteran of music videos, to direct the follow-up, "Eyes Without a Face." To make it even richer, I also shot it in 35mm. It was a much better video and went straight to number one on MTV's new video charts.

By then, I was well known in the video community. I was generally well liked by the artists and their management but hated by the record companies, who had to pay all the bills. Realizing that the MTV charts put music videos into a whole new league, I founded the Music Video Producer's Association (MVPA) and served as its first and longest president. It was one of those rare moments in time when we were in the forefront of cultural exchange, and it couldn't have been more exciting. But -- and there's always a but -- the workload and pressure were beginning to catch up with me.

In a pattern that would prove devastatingly consistent, my life in the music world came at the expense of a "normal" existence. I was too busy to work out, much less to pay attention to my personal life.

In truth, I just let all the little things go. I took my eye off the ball in my personal life and threw all my weight behind my professional, which is hardly the balance one needs in a good relationship. I told myself that I was focusing on the big picture. That was true, primarily because work was a lot easier to fix than my broken marriage. So even though my second child was about to be born, I did little, if anything, to prevent that marriage from falling apart.

On Halloween night, 1983, my wife and two friends were leaving a party when two drunks stumbled passed us. The smaller of the two, who was about three inches shorter than me, tossed a gallon jug of wine at my wife's feet.

I went after him as if I was in peak condition, which proved to be a mistake. Without even trying, he backed me up against a post and hit me at least six times before I could even get my arms up.

It was a shock and a huge blow to my ego (even though I'd later recognized him, in the sport's pages, as Hector Camacho, a future boxing world champion). I couldn't believe I had been beaten by a shorter, smaller man. As tough as it is for me to admit, I was more upset about that than I was about my marriage, which was collapsing.

Sensing it was beyond salvation, I decided the least I could do was regain control over my body. So I joined a gym in New York City and began the slow, painful process of putting my life and body back together again.

A Streetcar Named Desire

Although my relationship with Penny was in shambles, the music video business was booming. I had started to shoot jobs in New Orleans, because Louisiana was a right to work state and therefore posed fewer union problems.

That was important because even then, most music

videos usually had very low budgets. By working long hours in right-to-work states, we were able to create videos with higher production quality than we could have in places like Los Angeles or New York.

I met T'Boo, the woman who would become my second wife, on one of these shoots. Her real name was Lynn Allain Dalton, but her grandmother called her T'Boo, a Cajun nickname for *mon petit boo* (my little one).

Although we had never met, we grew up a few blocks from each other in uptown New Orleans. She had worked in commercials for my ex-brother-in-law, Tom Buckholtz, who had married my sister Ann for about 15 minutes, and was used to the long hours, travel, and stress of the commercial film industry. Sassy, bawdy, funny, and vivacious, she quite simply knocked me off my feet.

I had become close, personal friends with Billy Idol, who was also living in New York by then, so it was natural that T'Boo and Billy's girlfriend, Perri Lister, became friendly too. Before long, we were all inseparable.

That in itself was unusual, because most people in the music business base relationships, primarily, with an eye towards the business. Every once in awhile, though, you connect on a different level with the person beneath the persona. If that other person is a performer or a public figure, it becomes complicated, because it's like you're friends with two different people and have to act according to which one you're hanging out with at the time.

It was like that with Perri and Billy as the relationship evolved to more than just the business. We all had intersecting interests. Billy, who is much more intelligent and intellectual than his public image would have you believe, and I loved books and movies. Perri and T'boo loved shopping and parties.

When it was just us in private, it wasn't any different than hanging out with any other close friend. But as soon as we stepped into the public, he became Billy Idol and played his persona to the hilt. As soon as that happened, I became his buffer against the rest of the world.

Nightmares in Wax

In retrospect, I could have used more normal in my life, but in those early days of MTV, normal was hard to come by. Video had not just killed the radio star but birthed the video star. In attempts to top one another, excess became the status quo, with "normal" coming in a distant second.

Nowhere was this more evident than in the making of the video of the Jackson's song "Torture." One of the most expensive -- and one of the worst videos of all time -- the video was not only my *Heaven's Gate* but also a convincing demonstration of how desperate the Jacksons were to feed off Michael's runaway success.

What began as a relatively manageable three-day shoot somehow took a total of nine 20-hour days, topped off by a final day that went on for 36 straight, grueling hours. The irony of the whole extravaganza was that despite non-stop begging and pleading from Randy, Tito, and the others, Michael never showed up for the video.

Having met with Michael, who showed no interest in the project, I wasn't the slightest bit surprised by his absence. In fact, in anticipation, I had already rented a wax dummy of him from a Nashville wax museum and had flown it to New York.

It came in handy. All the shots of Michael in the video were actually the wax dummy with its arms up or down, which was about all the dummy could do.

Perhaps the only other interesting thing to come out of the video was that Randy fired the original choreographer, Billy's girlfriend, Perri Lister, and replaced her with his own girlfriend, a Lakers cheerleader named Paula Abdul.

Brave New World

In December, 1984, Penny and I divorced. She and the kids had moved to Connecticut. Convinced that everything was settled, I moved in with T-Boo in New York.

In retrospect, I moved too quickly. As much as I wanted to pretend things were ideal, they weren't. I had given Penny everything I could financially, which didn't sit well with T'Boo. And Penny, who considered T'Boo "the other woman," constantly undermined her to the children, who spent the weekends and summers with us.

I, sad to say, just passively sat there in the middle of it

all. I knew that there was a war waging around me, but it was easier just to escape into work. Picture Music was the new kid on the block and, as the biggest company of its kind, had all sorts of clout. I had 27 directors with me, relationships with the major labels, and the lifestyle of a rock star.

That frenetic activity may have distracted me from my domestic issues, but it ultimately became my undoing. With the best of intentions, I had let T'Boo become an integral part not just of my personal life, but of my professional one as well.

I knew that she resented Penny and understood why, but I didn't even realize she had started to resent me too. She thought I was hogging the spotlight and also holding her back from launching her own projects.

I should have noticed it, really, because there were enough small explosions and minor damage along the way. But when you're in that rock star fast lane, traveling all over the world, living in unimaginable luxury, partying and spending tons of money, you only look in the rear view mirror after someone rear ends you.

Welcome to Hollywood

At that point, T'Boo's resentments were still simmering, and I had other things to worry about. Like everyone else in the music video world, I was interested in making the leap from videos to film and, by 1986, was ready to cross that bridge. Hoping to launch Billy's movie career at the same time, the two of us met with

Joel Silver, who was riding the buzz off his recent film, *Streets of Fire*. On the plane to Los Angeles, we had come up with the idea of making a movie based on an article in *Rolling Stone* called "King Death," which in our heads would be a fictionalized analogy of Colonel Tom Parker and Elvis.

Joel thought it was a good idea, so he and I bought the rights for $5000 the next day and lined up pitch meetings with every studio in town. Each meeting went better than the last one. Captivated by the pitch and by the prospect of Billy as a film star, the executives were offering us development deals minutes after the meeting was over, as we were walking into to the next one.

By midday, Universal offered us a straight deal for a $10 million dollar picture (enormous at the time) with an additional million for a soundtrack. Knowing a good thing when we saw one, we cancelled the other meetings, thinking we had a movie.

And we probably would have, had it not been for Billy's manager, Bill Aucoin. Like most managers, he liked to control access to his "property" even when it was at odds with his talent's best interests.

It didn't help that he and I had been at odds ever since the "Eyes Without a Face" video. We were using dry ice, which posed a risk to a performer wearing contact lenses. I told Aucoin about the safety issues, but he just laughed and had Billy put them on.

Sure enough, the dry ice fused the contact lenses to

Billy's eyeballs, forcing him to cancel three upcoming concerts. The press got a hold of it, reporting that a video producer had blinded Billy Idol. Billy got a big kick out of that. Aucoin did not.

It also didn't help that Aucoin had developed a drug problem that only encouraged his paranoia over my role as the film's producer. Throwing up some fabricated objections to the soundtrack, he brought in Victor Drai, then a B-list producer, and said he was taking Billy and doing this movie with someone else.

The sole obstacle to the plan was the rights, which Joel and I owned. But Joel, disgusted and convinced the movie would never get made, wanted out. We took the high road and sold the rights back to Aucoin. But Silver was right. The movie would never get made.
Shortly thereafter, Billy replaced Aucoin with Freddy DeMann, a prominent California manager, and decided to move to Los Angeles. At the same time, my deal with EMI was starting to sour.

It wasn't because of anything EMI or I did. It was just that production companies have to be able to turn on a dime, and thus don't work well when locked into a major corporate structure. That's why film production companies are boutique agencies to this day.

To EMI's credit, they also knew it wasn't working, especially after the "Torture" video, and let me go. I opened up a new production company called Calhoun Productions, named after the street I was born on. (That street, I found out much later, was named after a famous Southern statesman who was also a notorious bigot. So much for historical references.)

I was still living in New York producing one video after another, but somehow T'Boo and I found the time to get married, in 1987, in New Orleans. It was a lavish, drunken, drug-fueled bash that lasted for four days.

Right after, we flew to England on a job. We didn't need a honeymoon, I reasoned, because I had already had one and our lives were one big honeymoon. But T'Boo had never had one. That would come back to haunt me later on.

In the meantime, I started spending more and more time with Billy in Los Angeles who was having management problems with Freddie Demann. I was still living in New York and running the company, so I was stretched pretty thin.

By then, the rap world was revolutionizing the music business and represented a huge opportunity in terms of music videos, most of which were shot in New York. I thought it made sense to hire a black director to shoot the rap videos, but everyone always wanted Scott Kalvert.

Ironically, Scott was a young, Jewish, speed/metal freak who hated rap music. But he had just won top honors for his video of "Parents Just Don't Understand," by Jazzy Jeff and the Fresh Prince, at the MTV Awards and was the name everyone wanted.

Together, Kalvert and crew did the hardcore stuff like Eric B and Rakim and Queen Latifah, which was shot in neighborhoods so bad that all of our clients carried guns and all our equipment disappeared. We did the moderate rappers like LL Cool J and the funny ones like Kool Mo Dee and the Fat Boys.

Suckerpunch

Although many of the rap videos came with challenges, the one that caused me the biggest headache was 1989's "I Think I Can Beat Mike Tyson."

It had been a big hit for DJ Jazzy Jeff & The Fresh Prince (Will Smith). At the time, Mike Tyson was the biggest athlete in the world. Our entire office and crew had been fans of Tyson since his New York City Golden Gloves days, so we were all looking forward to going to Don King's headquarters in Cleveland, where Tyson was training, to film the video's dream sequences.

The gym was really just steps away from King's main house, but Tyson drove his Ferrari full out from the house to the training area, which took all of a second and a half. As we were setting up, he'd step into the ring, and, out of nowhere, he'd hit anyone who was in there with him.

And, I mean hit. To the point where it hurt. Scott, the director, fled the ring nearly in tears when stalked by Mike. When he hit the cameraman, Dave Phillips, who was a big guy and carrying a full hand-held rig, Dave was fully ready to hit back, Panavision rig and all.
Afraid of damaging the equipment, we calmed Dave down and told Tyson to come back in an hour when we

were ready to film. So he got back in his Ferrari and drove back to the house.

We called him an hour later, but he kept us waiting for three hours. When he finally returned, he physically grabbed each of the girls on the set, forcing us to send them all into the motor home for their own protection.

The filming went fine until he lost interest. Fortunately, we got what we needed. But it was one of those times you found out your hero has feet of clay. After that afternoon, we all thought he had gone off the deep end and was heading for some serious jail time.

Celluloid Heroes

Although most of our work was on the music video "clip" (single song as opposed to a concert) side, I was increasingly interested in shooting concerts. It was simply a matter of creative satisfaction. Music videos were a director's medium. Producers, as the joke went, got none of the glory and all of the blame.

But in the concert business, the concert producer does almost all the creative work, and the director is the hired hand. So it was a natural progression for me to make.

It didn't hurt that the concert films were also potentially more lucrative than music videos, which had started to bottom out as an industry by the late 1980s. Budgets were high, but costs were astronomical. And, since everyone was using music videos to break into movies and commercials, the turnover was frustrating. So I decided to let T'Boo run the financial side of the business, including the clips we were doing, while I concentrated on the concert films.

Once again my timing was right. Before long, I was shooting all the big shows for superstars like Elton John, Cyndi Lauper, Pink Floyd, Dire Straits, Bruce Springsteen, Sting, Peter Gabriel, and Tom Petty for networks like HBO and MTV. We traveled to numerous exotic locations (industry slang for cheap Third World countries with horrible living conditions and human rights' violations), and socialized with the artists and their crews. There was no line between our professional and our personal lives. Caught up in the fable, we couldn't imagine living any other way.

Appetite for Destruction

It's no secret that the business is always stacked in favor of the big corporations, so it always felt good when you beat them at their own game. I was producing a segment for *Live at the Ritz,* MTV's Saturday night concert series, for $75,000 per episode, which was barely enough to cover our costs.

With that amount of money, we could only film the headliner. Normally that wasn't something that bothered me, but in 1988, Guns 'n' Roses was slated to open for the hard rock band, Great White.
It was early in their career, and Scott Kalvert thought they were going to be important and begged me to let him shoot them. To be clear, we had never shot the opening act. Even more pertinent, Kalvert wasn't directing the program. But I trusted him enough to take

him seriously and to run it by MTV. They told me it was out of the question, but, after I was paying for the tapes and Scott was shooting for free, they gave their okay.

The thing about Guns 'n' Roses even then was that you had to drag them on stage. Then they'd get so lost in their performance that you'd have to drag them off again. But when they were on, you could tell right away that they were the real deal.

I knew MTV would see it that way too. Sure enough, right on schedule, they called me a few days later. They admitted I was right and told me that they had decided to use the tapes after all.

I then had the pleasure of reminding them that, thanks to their own lack of interest, I owned the tapes and would happily sell it to them. They ended up paying me $150,000 for the footage.

It was one of those rare situations where everyone won. For the first and only time in my career, I got the best of MTV financially. And they ended up underpaying for what was to become the most popular concert show in the network's history. One they got to replay over and over again.

A View from the Bridge

As the '80s drew to a close, Billy's relationship with DeMann soured, so I introduced him to Tony Dimitriades. He was partners with Elliot Roberts, whose clients included Bob Dylan and Neil Young. In my opinion, Roberts was the best manager I'd ever worked with.

Right around then, Neil Young was putting together one of, if not, the first Bridge concerts, so it made sense that Tony would put Billy Idol and Tom Petty, who he also managed, on the bill. It was on Billy's birthday, November 30th, and Billy, who had been drinking, was in a great mood.

After he finished his set, we were hanging out in the dressing room celebrating. I got sidetracked in a bunch of conversations and wasn't paying attention to Billy's whereabouts until I heard the audience break out in a yell. Immediately I knew he had made his way back on stage -- right into the middle of Tom Petty's set.

With no warning, he hugged Tom, announced that they shared the same manager and he loved them. Then, to the amazement of the band and the audience, he wandered off the stage.

As soon as the Heartbreakers finished the set, Stan Lynch, the Heartbreaker's drummer, stormed into the dressing room, angry and looking for a fight. We managed to calm him down. I apologized to Lynch and the rest of the band, saying it was just drunken behavior, and forgot all about the incident.

A few months later, I was watching the video for Petty's "Into the Great Wide Open," in which Johnny Depp played a Billy look-alike as a "rebel without a clue." He even had a girlfriend (Gabrielle Anwar) who looked a lot like Perry Lister.

It shouldn't have been a surprise, because Tony had Billy spend an hour alone with Johnny Depp, right before the video was shot, as part of Depp's acting process. Even so, I was enraged by the nastiness of the caricature and made no secret of my feelings to Tony and to Tom.

They claimed I was reading things into the video that weren't there. But the implication was obvious, and my bad feelings lingered. It would be several years before I would work with Tom again.

Red Sails Take Me

In the meantime, my world was beginning to unravel. In addition to the continued tension between Penny, who had moved back to New Orleans, and T'Boo, my lavish lifestyle was soaking up every cent I had. Even worse, the IRS was sniffing around. Things were about to get worse.

Everything started to unwind on a Cyndi Lauper video, "Who Let in the Rain." I had known her since the early 1980s, when her video of "True Colors" was wildly over budget and in trouble. Not knowing what to do, her record company asked me to oversee her music video career, and flew the director, Andy Morahan, and myself to Hawaii just to meet her.
We had just checked into the hotel room when there was a knock on the door. I went to open it, but there was no one there. After this happened three times, I knew someone was playing a trick on me. So I waited by the door, looking through the keyhole.

Right before the person was about to knock, I opened it. Cyndi, who had been leaning over to knock, almost fell head first into the room. From that minute on, I knew we would be friends.

We worked together through three albums, culminating in the Grammy-nominated long form, *Cyndi Lauper in Paris*. By then, T'Boo and she had become friends. Knowing that Cyndi wanted to become a director and T'Boo a producer, I pulled away from my own role in the videos so that they could have their shot. It was well intentioned but ended up backfiring.

We were shooting it in New Orleans' French Quarter. It was a huge street scene with thousands of extras. Because there was nothing for them to do other than wait for crew, things started to get a little out of control.

T'Boo and Cyndi were in a production office on the other end of the square, so, worried about a potential riot, I grabbed a loudspeaker and started handling the crowd and restoring order.

In the middle of this, someone tapped me on my shoulder. It was the entertainment editor of *USA Today*, who happened to be in town on vacation and had stumbled upon the scene. She asked me if she could interview someone about the video for her paper, so I told my intern to go find T'Boo.

When we found out it would take at least 10 minutes to locate her, the reporter, who was on a tight deadline, told me she couldn't wait that long. Then, finding out I was the executive producer, she wanted to interview me on the spot. After she promised, she would identify T'Boo as the person in charge, I gave her a few quotes.

When the paper came out the next day, the front page of the entertainment section of *USA Today* explained how Cyndi Lauper had paralyzed the French Quarter for two hours, with quotes from producer John Diaz.

As soon as T'Boo saw it, she became angry beyond reason. Nothing I could say made her feel less betrayed. I probably could have seen her side of it better, but I felt unjustly accused and victimized.

The Nineties:
Live and in Concert

In those years, when David Dinkins was mayor, New York was in decline and becoming an increasingly dangerous and depressing place to live. After T'Boo was accosted on the subway on Halloween, 1989, I knew it was time to move back to California.

We got a realtor named Sharona (yes, THAT Sharona). She found us a great house in the Hollywood Hills. We moved in on January 1, 1990.

I kept the operation going in New York City and opened a secondary shop in LA. I continued to immerse myself in concert videos and films. After a year, I realized I didn't need the overhead of a production company, closed the office and hired myself out as a producer of international music events.
Since my resume already included the Grammy-

nominated show for Cyndi Lauper in Paris, an Amnesty International concert tour with Springsteen, Sting, and Peter Gabriel, Pink Floyd at The Palace at Versailles, and my personal favorite, Dire Straits at the Roman Coliseum in Versailles, it didn't take long to get work.

For one of my first projects, I flew up to Sacramento, where U2 was performing. I was going there to shoot a testimonial from Bono for a benefit concert for Kurdish Relief that he wasn't able to attend. I was also going to film the band singing "Until the End of the World," which I understood was about the Last Supper.

Before the taping, their tour manager asked me if I knew the meaning of the song. Since Easter was in a few days and I knew the band had Christian leanings, I surprised him with my answer.

We started talking, and that led to a discussion about Christianity. I told him that one of my favorite songs, "Mysterious Ways", seemed to be about The Blessed Virgin Mother, John the Baptist and the Holy Spirit, and showed him the Rosary (my father's) I always carried. He told me that U2's music was replete with religious references and that the meaning was in the "ear of the beholder."

He must have told the band about our conversation, which seemed to go a long way with them. Later, as I met with Bono to go over the taping and the message he would be delivering to the world in support of the Kurdish people who were on the verge of genocide, he was the perfect listener. The shoot went really well. And though the years had done nothing to diminish my belief that most benefit concerts are mostly expensive excuses for rich people to have fun, for once, the message was heard, as U2's song and Bono's words were high points of an extremely successful effort to raise awareness for the plight of the Kurds.

Leaving on a Jet Pack

Shortly after U2, I got two back-to-back projects that I knew would be historic. The first was a Michael Jackson concert film. The second was a tribute concert celebrating Bob Dylan's 30th year in show business.

Michael's job was first. HBO wanted to do a live show with Michael from Bucharest, Romania. It would be Michael's first live concert and the self-proclaimed "King of Pop" was justifiably paranoid about the concert and the political situation in Romania. It wasn't entirely his imagination -- there were huge bullet holes in the walls of our Hilton Hotel from the political turmoil they had just come out of.

The tour was not going to make it to the States, so we started in Munich and filmed three songs for Fox TV's American audience. We also filmed two shows at Wembley Stadium, as well as documentary footage backstage and on the road.

At Bucharest, we used 22 cameras to shoot the show. It went out live everywhere in the world but the States. This was all Michael's doing. He had never done a live concert before, and, since this was going to be the biggest television concert ever, surpassing even Elvis' legendary 1973 *Live from Hawaii* shows, he wanted it to be perfect for American television.

I understood the reasoning -- the live event had big risks associated with it -- but hadn't counted on how long it would take to edit it. I had to be in New York and start work on the Bob Dylan concert and estimated that I could clean up the footage at Rutt Video, my favorite editing facility, over four days.

I should have known better: I hadn't factored in Michael's nervousness or his ability to put everyone on what we called "Michael time." Or his insistence on staying in Neverland, where he felt he could better concentrate on the video, rather than coming to New York.

He cancelled three concerts so he could be available, and had us set up a downlink satellite, which enabled him to review the daily edits. Then, every night, in that soft- spoken voice of his, he would tear everything we had done that day apart and give us specific instructions on how to fix it.

By the second week of this four-day job, with no end in sight, we had taken over every room at Rutt and commandeered every CGI machine. The problem wasn't with his performance, which was fine, but with the audience, which he felt was lacking the proper enthusiasm. To get the audience response he wanted, he told us to use footage from the other audiences instead.

In today's world, that would be easy, but back then, it was a nightmare. The mixing towers in each of the cities had been draped with a banner with the name of the city. They were legible and in virtually every shot of the crowd. So each time we used the Munich or Wembley audiences, we had to hand paint Bucharest into each banner.

It was an endless chore, and as the HBO date got closer, my nerves were as bad as Michael's. Every night I'd beg him to hurry and get this done. And every day, he'd ignore me.

We didn't finish it until the morning of its broadcast premiere. I was about to show it -- finally -- to a group of HBO executives, who were waiting in the screening room. But just before the screening, Michael called and told me there was a problem.

The concert had ended with Michael flying off on a jet pack, and one of the horn players, who was also a radio DJ, announced, "Ladies and gentlemen, Michael Jackson has left the building." After watching the whole thing, Michael decided he hated the voice and wanted it changed.

I explained to Michael that the executives were waiting, and that we had no time to find someone with a better voice, much less to do all the paperwork required to secure their participation. But Michael just said, "No, Johndiaz. [He had always called me that, as if it were one word.] I love your voice. I want you to do it."

As the producer, I was legally allowed to be in it, so, in my best radio voice, I read the line. But he again told me no, that he wanted me to use my real voice. So there at the end of the most widely seen television concert in history, is my Southern accent, announcing that Michael had indeed left the building.

Knocking at Heaven's Door

The Bob Dylan concert, which was celebrating Bob's 30th year in show business in Madison Square Garden, was every bit as challenging. Driven by my good friend, Kevin Wall, it was a prestige event from the moment it was announced. We were flooded with offers from every legend in the world.

It's not a bad problem to have, but all of these stars were of a certain age and stature. There were none of the young talent who had grown up listening to Dylan, who, coincidentally, would broaden the appeal of the concert.

I raised the issue with G.E. Smith, of *Saturday Night Live* fame, who was the show's musical director. In a brilliant move, he had hired Booker T. and the MGs to be the house band, and I thought his television experience with breaking bands would make him sympathetic.

He immediately agreed, so we went to Bob. Since the lineup was already crowded, we knew we could only add one song. Thinking we could get two for one, we suggested Henry Rollins, who was then pioneering his spoken word act and being hailed as a young Bob Dylan, and Eddie Vedder, who was still somewhat unknown, performing "Masters of War" as a duet.

Dylan, who hadn't really shown concern about the

lineup until then, completely dismissed the idea. I argued that he needed some new guys on the stage. He nixed Rollins perhaps because the underground press was calling him a modern Dylan. In deference to G.E. Smith, however, he agreed to Eddie.

The day before the show, we had rehearsals in the basement of Madison Square Garden, and all these legends were there. Everyone was talking to each other except for one guy, standing all by himself. The way he was standing made it look like he had a spotlight trained on him, but it also seemed like he was trying to melt into the concrete.

Although he wasn't in the show, Billy had come to visit. Because the guy looked so lonely, Billy and I walked over and introduced ourselves. We chatted for a bit and then left. When we were out of earshot, Billy asked me if I had seen his eyes. I told him I wasn't going to say anything, but that yes, his eyes glistened and shone. To which Billy whispered one word: "Jesus."

Thus I met Eddie Vedder, who hours later, with rehearsals in full swing, got up, sang a verse, and knocked all these rock stars out. Neil Young was the first, running up to him and telling him how fantastic it was. Eddie would have probably been happy with a cursory hello. But this was not that kind of day. I remember thinking that I hadn't seen a room with that much love since Woodstock.

The next day, before the show, I went up to each artist and asked if they wanted to use a teleprompter. Everyone, including Dylan, said yes -- except for Eddie. It surprised me, because "Masters of War" was perhaps Dylan's most lyrically dense song, so if anyone could have used help, it would have been him. He must have picked up on my hesitation, because, with those uniquely shining eyes, he nodded yes.

I assured him I'd place the teleprompter in line with his natural head position and would hide it so that no one could see. Then I went into the pit, where I had a perfect view of his performance.

He didn't need the teleprompter. In fact, he sung the entire song without ever opening his eyes. Afterwards, the crowd -- both the audience and the artists -- went wild.

Knowing that Eddie had just stolen the show, Neil Young rushed up and gave him a big hug as he was leaving the stage. Later that night at the after-party he was the only relatively unknown person sitting a table with Dylan, George Harrison, Clapton, Neil Young, and Tom Petty. That was the night, I felt, that he became a genuine rock star.

For every winner, there is usually a loser. In this case, that role fell to Sinead O'Connor. Neither G.E. Smith nor I wanted to work with her, but Dylan was insistent that we use her.

I was angry, because she had recently cancelled a live global broadcast from Switzerland two hours before it was scheduled to air, leaving me holding the bag. And just a week before, as a guest on *Saturday Night Live*, she had ridiculed both Americans and the Pope, and got booed. To retaliate, she scrapped the song she had rehearsed (and cleared) and went into an acapella version of the Bob Marley song, "War."

Since the song had not been cleared for broadcast, the Marley estate had *SNL* by the short hairs and charged a fortune for the rights. As musical director, it had all come down on G.E.'s head, so he was in no mood to deal with her.

In deference to Smith, I agreed to let him leave the stage for her performance. I was sure I could handle her song, but when Sinead walked out, the entire crowd booed her again. The band kept trying to start the song, figuring she would be fine once she started to sing, but instead she quieted the band down and, on live television, started to go into the same Marley song. I could hear the Marley estate just licking their chops at another payday, but the crowd continued to drown her out and made her cry. To regain control, I had Kris Kristofferson go out and escort her off the stage, which he did in a gentlemanly, paternal way.

(From a personal standpoint, there was an upside in that the show was already running long, and this snafu had just saved me three minutes.)
In a concert packed with so many highs, there was a lot to look forward to, but as far as I was concerned,
I saved the best for last.

It had been a foregone conclusion that we would end with "Knocking on Heaven's Door," which Guns 'n' Roses had just had a huge hit with. But given the stature of the lineup, I didn't think that one encore, particularly such an obvious one, was enough. I argued that we needed a less expected lead into "Heaven's Door," and suggested the encore lead off with a version of "My Back Pages."

That song had been a smash for the Byrds, who had always been one of my favorite bands and the American band that probably did more to break Dylan than anyone else. They had more or less disbanded by the mid-1970s, but even though there were more famous people who could sing, I argued that we invite Roger McGuinn, the Byrd's lead singer. Dylan liked Roger, so that was that.

I also had a private reason for suggesting that song. One of my best friends and favorite musicians when I was growing up, Baldwin Justice, had sung it at every high school dance, specifically because he knew I loved it. Baldwin was killed in 1980 in an automobile accident in Mexico, and this was to be my silent homage to Baldwin.

Not that it affected the logic of the choice. "My Back Pages" has six different verses and Roger McGuinn took the first verse, followed by Tom Petty, Neil Young, Eric Clapton, George Harrison, and, finally, Dylan. Then they joined together for the final refrain. It was an unparalleled array of star power, but, standing in front of the stage, with tears rolling down my face, the only voice I could hear was Baldwin's.

Meltdown

The show was a tremendous success and led to more work than I could handle. I was flying all over the world with virtually every rock star in the book and loving it.

There was only one problem. While I was hobnobbing with the musicians, T'Boo was running around LA with nothing to do.

Although I didn't want to admit it, I had encouraged the situation. Thinking it would be better for both of us if we didn't work together, I had completely removed her from my business, with the idea that we needed more space. I fooled myself into thinking that this was simply a way of encouraging her to work on her own projects.

It didn't work out that way. Over the next six months, in front of an entire industry and friends, we self-destructed in the most public, embarrassing way possible. Even then, I'm ashamed to say, the breakup completely blindsided me.

True to form, ignoring the years of fast lane living and recreational drug use, encapsulated in the rock 'n' roll bubble, I neatly blamed everything on her. Then I fell apart.

Although I know now that I was paying the price for my lifestyle, back then I wallowed in self pity, depression and pain. I was emotionally exhausted, living mostly on borrowed money, and going through the worst year of my life.

Over the following months, I let everything go. My weight dropped from 168 to 118 pounds in three months. I lost my house, tried licking my wounds in New Orleans, and finally made my way back to Los

Angeles.

For the next six months, I holed up in Billy's place, only leaving his house for workouts at Gold's Gym in Hollywood or for long rides on our Harleys. Finally, I found an apartment in Venice Beach that was big enough for my kids to come and visit. I joined the Gold's in Venice and started lifting weights again.

And one day, I noticed this petite body builder with a fabulous physique, Nancy Louise Jones. Suddenly I had all the impetus I needed to get my life back together.

On the Road Again

I knew that the best thing I could do was go back to work. But the opportunity on the table was one I really didn't want to do. It was Woodstock II, and it represented everything about the music business I had come to hate.

It wasn't just that I was upset by the idea of "you can't go home again," or that this festival had nothing to do with the first one and was just about making money. It was also that I knew I was in no state to produce it, no matter how badly I needed the work. Luckily, my second, Allen Newman, was the producer, and it didn't take long for him to ask me to come on board and work under him. At the time, my ego thought he needed me to get him out of a jam. Only later did I realize that it was the other way around. Thanks, Allen!

There were about 11 of us who had been at the

original festival working on the second one, and we were constantly being asked for interviews. I turned every one of them down. I wasn't connecting with the event and wasn't happy to be there, so the last thing I wanted to do was talk about it.

An unexpected burst of violence changed all that. I got a call telling me to get to the second stage, where Green Day was performing. It had just rained, and there was mud all over.

It didn't take long for someone to throw a handful of mud on the stage. Rather than let it be, one of the Green Days stopped, picked it up, and threw it back at the crowd. "Oh, no," I thought. "You can't do that."

Sure enough, the stage was awash in mud. And rocks. One hit Billie Jo Armstrong, the lead singer, in the face, knocking a tooth out. The bass player was still throwing rocks back at the crowd, so this little tank of a security guard ran up to him and told him to stop inciting the fans.

Rather than listen to reason, the musician swung his guitar into the security guard's face. The security guard punched him with enough force to break the bass player's jaw. (The band sued him later and lost.)

The crowd, drunk with the scent of blood, went wild. And that was a glorious moment. Because here, amidst wholesale corporatization and commodification of everything in sight, the real spirit of rock 'n' roll was still alive.

It made me feel a lot better about being there. I went to see Traffic and The Allman Brothers, neither of whom had played at the original concert, and I was happy to be back.

Hitching Post

The road, while never easy, just gets harder as you get older. Thinking it was time to stay put, I put a lot of effort into producing a concert show for television. And in 1996, the same year Nancy and I got married, my dream came true.

PBS agreed to run *ON Tour*, a music series that ultimately would feature more than 100 artists, including Metallica, Ozzy Osbourne, and No Doubt. Although none of them fit the PBS mold of the time, the show won critical acclaim and ran for five years. But while an artistic success, it never became a big money maker.

With an eye towards my bank account, I was surfing AOL, one of the show's sponsors, one day in 1998, and stumbled across an article that talked about Z Company, a small San Diego operation that let people upload their own music to something called the Internet.

Digital Killed the Video Star

Z Company, the subject of the article, had already uploaded 20,000 garage bands, but there wasn't one I had heard of. Knowing that Billy wanted out of his contract with Capitol Records, I called Michael

Robertson, who ran Z Company, and told him that Billy Idol and I wanted to meet with him.

I'm sure he thought it was a joke, and was shocked when I came in with Billy. Their office -- two tiny rooms with six desks and servers everywhere -- was housed in the General Atomics facility, a huge corporate campus in Del Mar for nuclear scientists. We immediately liked Robertson, who was 29 and soft spoken. Before we left, Billy gave him several unreleased songs to put up and download free of charge as a Christmas present to his fans.

It was simply a ploy to get Capitol Records' attention, and it worked. Even though it was 1998, when the idea was still a relative novelty, the songs were downloaded more than a quarter of a million times in a few days. Around about then, Billy's manager, Tony Dimitriades, woke me up at six in the morning, yelling at me through the phone to take down those songs.
Although, it could have been done with a click, I knew he didn't understand the technology and stalled him by saying the process would take three days. That gave us enough time to make the story big enough to catch Tom Brokaw's attention. After interviewing Billy on the NBC Nightly News, he ended up praising him for having the guts to defy the record companies and champion an emerging technology.

The tactic worked. After a very angry Capitol Records dropped Billy, I became convinced that the future of music was on the Internet. To get in on the ground floor, I convinced Michael to let me work there. First, I was an unpaid consultant and, later, as an executive paid primarily in stock.

The new name of the company, MP3.com., was an immediate hit with investment bankers, who couldn't stop throwing money at us. Michael brought in a new president, Robin Richards, and before you had realized what had happened, we had 11 million dollars in the bank and a company roster of 300 (which was 20 times more than what we started with). By July of 1999, we went public, raising close to half a billion dollars. Such was the hype and glamour of that first Internet bubble.

2000: A Space Odyssey

Tony, who managed both Billy and Tom Petty, was now totally on board with the value of "illegal downloads" and gave me new material from Tom as well. The record companies, however, were far more threatened by us and waiting to take us to court.

They didn't have to wait long to find the reason. In 2000, Michael created the predecessor to the cloud, which he called a locker service. In what was extremely cutting edge at the time, he made it possible for someone to upload their music library onto the Internet and listen to it whenever and wherever they were online.

The only problem with the idea was that it took up to 20 minutes to upload a single song. Instead, Michael wanted to store a digital copy of every song ever recorded on a server. That way, as soon as someone entered the CD's name, the server would recognize the CD and immediately store it as a digital copy, without ever having to download the music.

In Michael and the company lawyer's minds, a digital copy was really just stored ones and zeroes and not the same thing as a physical piece of recorded music. I didn't buy that argument or the idea that the artists would benefit from the wholesale and, to my mind, illegal wholesale uploading of music. Instead, I argued that we should test the waters by uploading only a few songs. That way, we'd be protected against a huge copyright lawsuit.

Those objections were viewed as reactionary, so with Michael's blessing, each of the by now 500 MP3.com employees were frantically uploading every album that they could get their hands on. Within two weeks, they seemed to have found every piece of music that had ever made its way out of a recording studio.

Just as I had warned, every record label and publisher in the business sued us. Worried that I would be forced to testify that I had argued against the uploading, the company decided to send me on the road, where I'd be out of reach of the prosecution.

I couldn't help feel marginalized; my role in the company shifted. As Michael was spending a fortune settling these lawsuits one at a time, I set about in my new role, which was to turn MP3.com into the first truly global music site. In my mind, these sites would be able to reflect their own scenes and cultures, in their own language.

My experience touring and producing videos in Japan and the Far East convinced me that Asia was the most fertile place to launch a site like MP3.com. I went to

Japan, Korea, Taiwan and even into China. By October 2000, I was on target to finalize plans for MP3.com/Japan and MP3.com/Taiwan.

My first stop was Japan. I had learned enough about Asia to understand the benefits of travelling with your own interpreter. Mine was Erik Newton, a young MBA with a specialty in business development. He was married to a Japanese woman, had lived and worked in Japan, and was fluent both in Japanese and Kongi, which is the basic alphabet all Asian languages spring from. In addition, he was also able to quickly devise business plans consistent with the underlying technology of the Internet.

The Japanese meeting went off without a hitch, as did the one in Taiwan. After three days of meetings with Rock Records, on October 31, we were ready to sign a deal there too.

PART TWO

Icarus Descending

Bulletproof

Remember,
When I was bulletproof?
Nothing could hurt me
Not even the truth.

Then I grew older,
But wiser, no way,
I longed for tomorrow
And lived for today.

Riders on the Storm

During the meetings, we kept hearing about a typhoon approaching the island. Since most of the people we were dealing with spoke English and were friends of mine, Eric's kids were intent on having him home for Halloween, so I told him I could handle the final meeting and put him on an early flight back to Los Angeles.

I spent that morning sitting in the hotel, watching the typhoon, named Xiang Xing, as it approached the coast of Taiwan. The weather was already bad enough to conduct the meeting on the phone, rather than in person. By 11 that morning, the weather was worse. I called my travel agent, my cousin Brian Diaz, and told him we might have to make changes to my schedule.

Then, as if by instinct, I began tracking the storm. When you're raised in New Orleans, tracking storms becomes a way of life. As a kid, I had run through the eyes of hurricanes, had palm trees crash through my roof, and helped clean up a devastated Mississippi coast. So spending the day watching it on CNN in the Hotel Shangri-La in Taipei, Taiwan, was something I would have done even if I weren't flying that night.

As news of the approaching typhoon continued, I became increasingly concerned about the Singapore Airlines' flight taking off as scheduled. I kept bugging the concierge for updates, and he kept telling me everything would be all right and that the flight would leave on time.

I trusted him, so I killed the day and left the hotel for the airport around eight o'clock that evening. The storm's outer reaches had touched down on the island, and the wind and the rain made the short drive into an hour ordeal.

By the time we got to the airport, the wind was so powerful that I could barely open the cab's door. The rain was falling in sheets, making it impossible to see. The wind, which seemed to be coming from the side, rather from up above, was powerful enough to trigger the automatic mechanisms on the doors to the airport, which were swinging wildly back and forth.

To stop them swinging, the mechanics at the terminal disconnected the doors. It stopped them from swinging, but it also destroyed their ability to act as a barrier. Now that they were wide open, there was nothing to stop the rain from pouring into the terminal.

I was carrying two bags. One was a rolling garment bag with clothes, and the other was a new leather bag, which housed my computer, cell phone, workout gear, books, and business materials. The woman behind the ticket window, still convinced that the plane would take off on time, directed me to the first class and club lounge.

Sure enough, around 10:30, we started preparations to board. I called Nancy and joked that I was taking a flight in weather that she would never fly in. She begged me to wait out the storm, but I told her that the officials told me that this type of weather wasn't unusual and that the plane would be fine. Then I said goodbye, hung up, and got ready to go through passport control.

Just as I showed my passport and papers to the agent, the power went out. It took them ten minutes to get the generators on line, minutes I thought would cause me to miss the plane. So when I finally got my passport stamped, I ran through the terminal to the gate and then ran to get to the plane. Little did I know that it would be the last time I would ever run again.

As I boarded the plane, the wind was shaking the 747 as if it were a toy. One of the Singapore flight attendants, a female dressed as a Geisha, seemed to be quite upset. On the way to my seat, the first seat on the left lower deck in the nose of the plane, she just kept repeating "oh, wind" over and over.

I gave a male flight attendant the suitcase with the clothes in it and my jacket and kept the smaller bag with me. The female flight attendant handed me a glass of water. I put my bag in front of me on the floor, belted myself in, then waited for her to come back and check that we were ready for take off. Instead, in record time, we started to taxi out of the gate. I looked through the window but couldn't see anything.

We taxied for a bit, made a sharp left turn, and immediately picked up speed. With my eyes glued to the window, I kept cinching my seat belt tighter and tighter. As we approached take off, I felt a large bump that seemed to come from the back of the plane. Then the plane seemed to rise up off the ground.

Within seconds, there was a substantial cracking sound that left an eight-inch hole under the window before raking down the plane's left side. Next came a huge jolt as the plane hit the ground right beneath me. Then all hell broke loose.

The plane started to disintegrate in front of me. The wall separated from the floor right next to my feet. My seat partially unbolted from the floor and twisted to the right. In one motion, I unbuckled my belt and jumped up, barely avoiding a huge fireball that was coming down the aisle like some special effect in a movie.

As flames washed through the cabin, I stayed behind the seat, using my bag as protection against the balls of jet fuel that were spewing and igniting everywhere. Oddly, I was not surprised or shocked or even scared. Instead, I had the most surreal crystal clarity.

I watched the video screen in front of me melt and could almost hear my brain simultaneously processing multiple thoughts, such as "I need my bag" and "I'm already dead," juxtaposed against images of my parents, my wife, my children, my friends and my family.

By the time I looked around, milliseconds, really, I saw a group of people rush to the door. I picked up my bag as the cabin filled with thick, black smoke. Unable to make much out and choking on the smoke, I followed the little emergency lights that lined the aisle and stumbled blindly to the door.

Which would not open. To force the door open, I hit it

with everything I had. I was prepared to jump, regardless of how high we were from the ground, so I was shocked to see the door pop out just inches above the ground. I pushed the person on my left out and helped another.

Then, as the heat licked my back and I started to fall through, the slide chute automatically deployed. But without anywhere to go, it bounced back and exploded, hitting me like an airbag right in the chest and face.

Tangled up in shards, I was propelled back into the plane and thrown up against a metal partition that was right behind the door. Looking to my left, I could see into the business class section, where people were sitting in their seats, burning to death.

What seemed to be an elderly Asian gentleman ran from the business class section to within inches of me, totally aflame from head to foot. His expression was not one of fear, pain or anger, but of wonder and astonishment. It was almost as if he had just had the epiphany of a lifetime and that it was glowing beautifully in the embers on his serene features.

I took it to mean that I was dead, and, like the Burning Man, I just didn't realize it yet. Globules of liquid fire continued to ignite everything in their path. Metal was melting like wax figures put to a blow torch. I wondered why I didn't melt and became even more convinced that I was dead.

By then, the black smoke was still thick but not enough to obscure the horror of the writhing, tortured figures trapped in their seats and burning as if they were already in Dante's Inferno. To this day, I don't know whether it was a trick of all the explosions going on, but some of those unfortunates had beautiful, radiant white light leaving their bodies and flowing upwards. It was, in the full glory of the word, awesome to see.

Moving instinctively, I struggled free from the plastic of the chute, and helped grab an older woman who had also been caught up in the shards. Together with six others, we ran to a spot about 200 feet from the plane. As we looked back, the plane was cloaked in huge plumes of flames and thick, black smoke. We couldn't see the back of the plane, which had broken off, or the only other person who escaped from his upper business class seat. At the time, we thought we were the only survivors.

My memories get hazy after that. I was clearly in shock but had enough coping skills to retrieve my phone from the bag and call my Dad, Nancy, and Robin Richards, to assure them I was all right. A van, which definitely was not an emergency vehicle, approached us from far away and finally picked us up. They dropped us at a small triage room on the terminal's ground floor. About ten or twelve others, in various states of distress, straggled in as well.

I thought at first that except for lung damage, a painful arm and shoulder, bruises in my lower body, and some burned knuckles, I was, miraculously, all right. I called Nancy back, and she asked me if this wasn't just one of my bad jokes. I told her it wasn't and said goodbye, because a distraught man whose traveling companions had died in front of him needed the phone to call the mother of one of the victims he was traveling with.

At some point we found out that the rear third of the plane, which had broken off on impact and ended up in a ditch, had caused a variety of injuries but no fatalities. There were still no ambulances, so crews near the plane tried to help those survivors through the wind and the rain, as some flight crews from China Air and I walked around the triage room trying to help.

It was a mess. One American male was burned from head to foot. He had no hair left, and his clothes were scorched to his skin. He was walking and speaking coherently but looked awful. A woman I had helped died right in front of me. An older man lay unconscious, while a child with a bad cut and burn down one leg and a gash on his hand sat in shock with his father. I went over and applied pressure to the wound, screaming for medics to come over and assist the child. When they finally did, they discovered an even more serious wound in his legs. I never found out if the boy survived or not.

I lent my cellphone to anyone who wanted to use it until we were loaded into a primitive ambulance and taken to the hospital. The hurricane was in full force by then. I remember screaming at the driver to slow down, that I hadn't just survived a plane crash just to be killed in an emergency vehicle on the way to the hospital. It didn't do a bit of good.

By the time we got there, the hospital was in utter chaos, with a line of people waiting to be admitted. I knew I was hurt, but I didn't trust the hospital and was determined to get back to America as quickly as possible.

Long past caring about propriety, I fired obscenities at the press, who had arrived in droves and were wandering freely among the survivors, sticking cameras into the horribly wounded faces. In full meltdown, I demanded whoever would listen to get me a cab.

I must have made enough of a nuisance of myself for a doctor convinced a cab driver, who was in the hospital waiting out what was now a full-fledged typhoon, to take me back to the Hotel Shangri La. The fare back to the city was $500.

Three other people joined me in the very scary ride back to the hotel. As we were literally sliding across water, CNN, who had gotten my number from my sister, called me up and said that my account differed from the official information they were getting.

According to those early reports, no one had been killed or even seriously injured. After a short preliminary conversation, they realized their information was false and put me on the air live, to describe what I had seen.

And thus began my 15 minutes of fame. Although I had never been shy around the press and had done my share of interviews, I had always tried to leave the outsized ego to the rock stars I worked with. But the plane crash changed all that and drew the media to me like flies to a racetrack.

I understood why. Despite my inability to move well -- something I dismissed as "normal" consequences of a high-impact accident -- I wasn't so gruesomely burned to be untelegenic. And my information so directly contradicted the official reports of "a minor plane crash" that they knew they had stumbled onto a big story.

Whether the weather or the driver's incompetence was to blame I'll never know, but we got lost several times on the way to the hotel. By the time we made it into the hotel, every joint in my body hurt terribly. Stuck in the position I had been placed in, I had to be helped from the cab and was having trouble walking. Luckily, several executives from Rock Records were already there to greet me and help me get to my room.

I'll never forget the CEO's tears as he somehow tried to apologize for all that had transpired, as if it was his fault. I tried to calm them down, which was backwards considering what I had just been through. But they were extremely upset that this happened on their soil for a meeting that they had called. And I was in shock.

After a while, thinking I needed sleep, they left. But I was afraid to close my eyes because of what I would see in my head. So instead of sleeping, I spent the next two hours shaking violently. Then I spent hours calling family members and close friends, just to let them know I was alive. Safe. A survivor.

And dodging journalists clamoring for interviews.

There were too many to keep up with, so I asked the front desk to screen all my calls. Around nine A.M., a junior executive for Rock Records came by to see if there was anything he could do. His p.r. skills took over, and he quickly sorted out the numerous interview requests.

As that was happening, Singapore Airlines seemed intent on heaping insult onto injury. They set up house in the lobby of the hotel, which had become crash central. Ostensibly they were looking after our needs, but they really were trying to get survivors to agree to a $25,000 payout and minimize their exposure and fallout from the crash.

This did not sit well with me, so I found myself talking to all the big morning and evening news shows not just in the US, but in England, Japan, and wherever there was someone who wanted to listen.

You Can't Go Home Again

By the time I left Taiwan several days later, on November 2, I still could barely walk. I continued to do the occasional interview, a full spread in *People* magazine being the most notable, after getting back to Los Angeles, but I generally avoided the press to focus on my injuries, which were more extensive than I had thought.

The first MRI showed that my entire body had compressed and that all my joints and tissues were swollen. It was obviously bad, but the doctors felt they couldn't fully assess the damage that had been done until I started to heal.

Although I wasn't overly concerned, the lead doctor, a young, handsome native of Thailand, suspected that the physical damage was substantial and that the mental trauma was even worse than that. He asked Nancy if she were prepared to deal with this. She replied with her usual spirit, saying, "Are you kidding? I'm bionic." Had she known what was in store, she might have responded differently.

Mother's Little Helpers

Because I hadn't really slept in three days, my first prescriptions were for Halcyon, a powerful sleep inducing drug, and Prozac, which took the edge off my fuel-injected, adrenalized state. A second doctor brought the opiates, including Percocet, Vicodin, Oxycontin, and Norco, for the pain. Although I was getting the highest dosages allowed, none successfully slowed down my mental state or quelled the pain. But they did make it very easy to get lost in a mental fog.

After a few weeks, my shoulder, which had probably been injured when I rammed into the plane's closed door, was the only part of my upper body that was still painful. My lower body, however, was a different story. Everything from my hips to my toes hurt. The only way I could walk was with a bent-over, shuffling gait, for which Billy nicknamed me Quasimodo.

Everyone but Nancy couldn't believe how well I was doing, but that was because she was the only one who had to deal with the screaming nightmares from which

I'd wake up 15 feet from the bed, crawling on the floor, trying to hide from the vivid images of the plane crash that haunted me as soon as I closed my eyes.

Sometimes I didn't even have to wait until night. These flashbacks, which sent me straight back into the burning plane, could strike at any time of the day. I saw Burning Man's reflection in store windows. I thought he was a cab driver or even a pilot, or, at odd moments, someone in a movie I had gone to. He'd even pop up unexpectedly in the middle of a business meeting.

I'd also see him whenever I traveled. He was in the airport at LAX, walking down the streets of Tokyo, or lurking at the mall. He always looked exactly the same, with that sense of wonder on his face as he burned. No one else noticed him, of course. It was enough to make me think I was going crazy.

Nancy thought I should just go up to him and tell him to go away. I laughed the suggestion off, thinking that he was not inclined to just disappear. I knew it was going to be up to me to make him go away, but I wasn't sure how or when to make that happen. The difficulty originated, I realized later, in my past and in particular to my relationship with Poppa, my grandfather.

Poppa

Poppa was my hero growing up. Short and compact, he was a brawler, a tough little guy, and I got all my toughness from him.
That's not to say I didn't love my dad. He was the best. I got pretty much all my discipline, my focus, and

everything else good about me from him. But he had a wicked temper, which I inherited. It was Poppa who taught me what to do with it.

Every summer, he'd take Momma and us kids to Mexico. On this particular summer, when he was about 56 years old, my dad had rented a truly spectacular house about an hour outside Mexico City. Set high up in the mountains, it was built on four levels on the side of a gorge and overlooked the majestic Popocatepetl, one of the world's most active volcanoes.

There was a swimming pool on the lowest level, a guest house on the second, a garden on the third and a main house on the fourth. There was a huge yard with a lonely but beautiful lemon tree in its middle. And there were servants, making it impossible to feel anything but really rich.

Daddy, who was an eye, ear, nose, and throat doctor, had to stay in New Orleans working for most of the summer but would visit every now and then.

That was the summer Poppa embarked on a fitness kick and took up running, swimming, and working out. Lost in hero worship, I was more than happy just to follow his lead. I was the only one.

My dad happened to be at the house on that summer night, the night no one in my family ever talks about. I shared a room with Poppa. We had bunk beds. I slept on the top, and Poppa slept on the bottom. That night, saying he didn't feel well, he turned in early, almost at the same time I did.

He coughed and gagged all night long. It was so loud and so constant that I couldn't fall asleep. Periodically I asked if I shouldn't get my father, but Poppa kept telling me he was okay and not to bother my dad. At some point I fell asleep, and, at another point during that sleep, Poppa died, the victim of a heart attack, right there, underneath me in the bottom bunk.

(All my life, I've thought he would have lived had I only gone to my dad. Ever since, I've had trouble sleeping and still revert to a weird sleepless mode when I'm rattled.)

A few days later, we had a memorial service in the cathedral in the Mexican square for him. I had been an altar boy who had served numerous masses for the dead by then, but this time, I saw bright red blood dripping out of the corner of his coffin onto the stone floor of the Cuernavaca cathedral. I thought that it was Poppa, still alive and trying to get out.

That weird vision stayed with me ever since. And it was the only one that I had ever had until Burning Man. It wasn't lost on me that Burning Man, however Asian, somehow resembled Poppa, or that these visions were a symptom of post-traumatic stress disorder.

Not that the observation helped. As I was to find out, unless you were a military casualty, there were very limited resources devoted to PTSD available to you. Besides, these paralyzing hallucinations took a back seat to my physical condition, which, despite all efforts, was degenerating.

At first, I just limped along but ended up having to use crutches and a wheelchair. It didn't stop me -- I was still working and traveling like a crazy person -- but part of me already knew I was digging myself into an even deeper hole.

Road Tripping with Burning Man

A few months after the crash, as part of a story *48 Hours* was doing on me, I agreed to go back to the site of the accident. The debris from the plane was still sitting on the runway and would remain so until the final investigation was completed. There was virtually nothing left of the plane from the nose to where the tail end had broken off. As I looked at it, I couldn't believe that I had survived.

That experience was part of a larger trip -- part business and part personal -- that was to take me to Tokyo (for business) and Thailand, to buy an urn for Nancy's mother's ashes. I had also decided to say my goodbyes to Burning Man, whose appearances had been triggering increasingly disturbing hallucinations.

One of the most upsetting of those took place in the movies, where he was least welcome. I've always liked to go to the movies by myself and was looking forward to watching *Hannibal* at a theater on the Santa Monica Promenade. I bought some popcorn and walked through the theater doors. I let my eyes adjust to the cool darkness and comfort of the movies and hobbled up to the front, where I like to sit.
Before I could get very far, the door slammed open, discharging a rather large woman in a hurry to find a

seat. She must not have seen me in the dark theater, because she ran over me like a bowling ball. I landed on my hands and knees, and wham, I was right back in the airplane. There were the same lights in the aisle, the same seats on each side.

And like the airplane, everything and everyone seemed to burst into flames. Several people, including the woman who knocked me down, came to my aid, but, thinking that they were engulfed in flames, I refused their help.

Eventually the flashbacks subsided enough for me to let one man help me up. I waddled over and tried to watch the movie, but Burning Man came and sat next to me, bringing with him surreal images of the interior of the plane.

After that, I realized I had to do something about the hallucinations and was convinced the time to do it was in Taipei, where we had met. From there, I planned on going to a beach resort, where I could figure out my next moves in relative peace and solitude.

First, though, I had to come to grips with the fact that airplanes were going to be different for me from now on.

I had always been a fearless flyer and had never given the process a second thought. On my way to Tokyo, however, I read the safety guides backwards and forwards. I checked out the escape routes and the emergency lights. I looked at doors long and hard, studying how to open or disarm and release them.

(I still do that to this day. I probably know more about the plane than the flight attendant. If I see something I don't understand, I ask them to check with maintenance or whoever has the proper answer. I don't stop until I get the answer.)

I noticed that this particular plane had fairly standard doors that open out and off to the side. The release mechanism to remove the door completely was right inside the wall at the hinges. The chute was armed after takeoff. The panel to disarm it was fairly well displayed. The escape lights were on the seats, rather than the floor. I was six paces to the nearest exit and another five paces to the door across from it. This was the most important information since there is not much time in the chaos of a plane crash for you to get out.

(I could go on, but you get the picture. It's important, because most accidents happen on takeoff or landing. You can up your odds just by being prepared and ready to act quickly. As I said, though, you get the picture.)

The flight to Tokyo was relatively uneventful. Burning Man had left me alone on it, but I saw him frequently in Tokyo. Because I had expected to see him there, he didn't disturb me much. The two of us went to Viet Nam, shared a suite at the Bangkok Oriental, and then we were on to Phuket, an island beach resort in Thailand. After that, we were going to Taipei, which was where I planned to say our goodbyes.
Taipei seemed to be the natural end of the line for us. I had come to regard him as a restless spirit looking for home and thought that he'd find the peace we were

both missing there. I warned him about it, but he didn't say anything. Instead, like usual, he just burned. The same look as always was on his face, his widespread eyes and his features, the light grey hair on his head.

Phuket itself was an unexpected side trip. Even though I had never even heard of it before, I felt driven to go there. I noticed that Burning Man was driving the cab to the Bangkok airport and worried that he'd also be flying the plane. But, luckily, he rode in coach. I saw him go by after I sat down. He didn't wave. He just burned.

When I got to Phuket, I couldn't explain why, but felt like I was meant to be there. I spent five days at the resort, slept well for the first time since the crash, and never saw Burning Man. Not even once. Towards the end of my stay, during a furious thunderstorm, I ended up in a random, intense conversation with the chef, David Hamilton. For some reason, I blurted out that I was at Phuket recovering from a plane crash.

"Oh, the Singapore Airline Flight 006," he said. He went on to say that the CEO of the resort was on the board of Singapore Air, and that a number of guests had been on that flight. Memories of it , he assured me, were still fresh.

As soon as he told me, everything made sense. Burning Man had brought me here. Although I couldn't prove it, I had this idea that he had lived here and led me back to his home.

No Fool like an Old Fool

Although that was the end of Burning Man, it was hardly a return to normal. I still was in intense pain, still suffered from PTSD, and still hadn't gotten a definitive assessment of the extent of my injuries.

In the meantime, to deal with the pain and the PTSD, I had secretly increased my intake of opiates and psychotropic (mind-altering) drugs. On top of that, work had become increasingly stressful.

MP3.com had been settling lawsuits with the record companies, but it ate up half the cash we had raised. The stock price had dropped from $104 to five dollars a share. And we had no revenue to sustain us. So, in 2001, with the Internet boom looking like a big bust, we were bought for $400 million by Vivendi, a rich French water and waste-management company whose CEO wanted to be in the entertainment industry.

Then he bought Universal, which included its TV, movie and music business, as well as Universal Records. As he tried to integrate our digital platform into his otherwise Internet-resistant company, he realized they'd need more than a billion dollars to make the effort worth their while. So, figuring it was cheaper to write us off, they began dismantling MP3.com.

That was a real shame, not to mention a short-sighted mistake. Michael Robertson had never intended to become a music entrepreneur. He had always envisioned MP3.com becoming a social site where regular people could come and post snapshots of their own life on their page of the Internet. If that sounds like Facebook, it's because it was.

If that's not enough of a wasted opportunity, we were also getting ready to launch MP4.com, which was devoted to videos. Two years later, the guys at YouTube not only had the same idea but were able to execute it. Ironically, the billion dollars they had thought was too expensive would have made them one of the most powerful and visionary companies of the 21st century.

Which goes to say that I left MP3.com in 2002, with nothing financial to show for my time. To compound the problem, Singapore Airlines, rather than pay off millions of dollars in damages to us, threatened to tie us up in court for the next ten years. Rather than fight them, I had quickly settled with them for a fraction of what I should have received.

Had I known then how badly I was hurt and how difficult it would be to recover, I would have held out. By this time, I had several different specialists, one per problem. No one could diagnose the exact nature of the degenerative problems in my lower body, but each one had a different pill for my physical pain and mental woes.

All I knew was that my lower body was in constant pain. I couldn't walk anymore without crutches or a wheelchair. And I couldn't function for more than two or three days without having to spend one or two days flat on my back.

Eventually, the doctors had decided I had a massive "stretch injury," or, in other words, a whiplash to the lower spine, complicated by scar tissue that had formed around the damaged nerves in my back. To ease the pain, they continued to prescribe different kinds of pills. They didn't work but were addictive just the same.

On top of that, my lifetime of recreational drug use convinced me that I knew more than the doctors about drugs and could do a better job at the dosages than they did. Since the drugs were readily available on the streets of Los Angeles and Tijuana, I decided to take matters into my own hands.

In 2004, I began buying the opiates on the black market and taking two or three times the recommended dosages, just to escape from the pain. Around then, I also started taking a milder opiate, Tramadol, under a doctor's prescription but at five times the recommended amount.

I wasn't stupid -- I knew I was playing with fire -- but it felt so good to be walking and moving around that the prospect of addiction seemed worth it. Besides, I thought I could fool everyone. No matter how out of control I was inside, I (thought I) remained funny and affable. And when I wasn't, people would just put it up to the emotional upheaval caused by the aftermath of the crash.

Until I had a breakdown, and my secret came out. It started, as it often does, with a stupid argument I was having with Nancy and my son, Holland, about who -

Tyson or Holyfield - bit whose ear. I kept trying to say Tyson, but I ended up saying Holyfield.

After they kept saying "no," I went nuclear and started screaming that I had slept with all of Nancy's friends, a massage therapist, and a tall black man. None of it was true, and it came out of nowhere. I remember feeling detached from my body, watching me make up all this stuff. I asked myself what I was doing but couldn't stop myself.

Paying the Piper

Finally they calmed me down. As my drug habits became clear, they became, appropriately, horrified. Through a family friend, Dr. Sue Smalley, they got in touch with Dr. Laura Audell, a specialist in pain management, who agreed to see me immediately.

Working with a pharmaceutical psychiatrist, Dr. Bernard Bearman, she began managing all the drugs that were being prescribed by my team of doctors. She replaced all the opiates I was taking with 80 mg of methadone, taken in a cocktail that included some psychosomatic drugs Dr. Bearman prescribed.

Methadone is not undertaken lightly; most people stay on it all their lives. But it seemed to be the best way to get me off the opiates, so I agreed. And it did work, controlling the pain enough to make me want to make a comeback.

In true rock 'n' roll fashion, I got a sidecar for my motorcycle, went on tour with Billy a few times, and went to the 25th Anniversary of MTV. It was all familiar, comfortable territory and was, I thought, just what I needed.

While I was enjoying being back in the music world, Nancy embarked on an architectural adventure. We lived in a three-story apartment Frank Gehry had designed, but I couldn't navigate the steps. Nancy had always dreamt of building something grand, so we bought a big lot and started construction on our mansion.

The house was designed by Frank Fitzgibbons. A 5,000 square foot metal and glass extravaganza that sat on a 17,000 square foot lot about two miles from the beach, it was a huge critical and artistic success. But I hated it from the beginning, because it made me feel like I was trapped in a beautiful, sterile museum. Although there was more space than I knew what to do with, I spent most of my time in a small room next to the bathroom.

As custom-built mansions always do, it was also draining a lot of money from our account. Thinking I should go to work to pay for it, I started a new company, Wiwow. It was based upon the concept of using an at-the-time unheard of wi-fi download speed of four minutes on a specially developed wireless network located in airports that allowed you to rent or download a movie before you boarded the plane.

Thinking it was a great idea, I got a Chicago-based group called Concourse to invest in the project. Everything was going great -- they had contracts with

50 airports and were busily developing the model. But then Concourse, was bought out by Boingo, a firm that was developing wireless networks.

They liked the idea but wanted to focus on their own model and pulled the funding. I was on all kinds of drugs, so, in my delusional rock star fashion, I broke my own cardinal rule of business. Rather than look for other investors, I decided I was bulletproof and should just use my own money.

I then compounded the error by sticking the company with the lavish tab for my travels and lifestyle. Instead of curtailing my expenses and curbing my lifestyle, I lived the same way I always had, figuring the company would pay the tab.

By 2006, the bills were mounting, and the company, not to exclude myself, was falling apart. Although the idea was sound and we were moving ahead with the launch, we needed more money to continue. And I was in too much pain and too high to either raise the money or run a business.

Much of the high was coming from a muscle relaxant called SOMA, that replicated the high I used to get from opiates. I liked the feeling, but the combination of pain and drugs, including massive amounts of Tramadol, put me in a comatose state for 24 to 36 hours every two to three days.

To help Nancy disassociate herself somewhat from my day-to-day life, I hired an assistant, Teresa Poy, to work with me on Wiwow. Like Nancy, she witnessed the horrible flashbacks and my collapses and was convinced it couldn't go on. She finally dragged me back to Dr. Audell and demanded that something be done for me.

To get me off the the pills, the doctor suggested a new medical surgical procedure that inserted an electrical implant called a spine stimulator that controlled certain kinds of debilitating pain.

There was even a simple test, involving nothing more than poking a hole in the base of your spine and pumping electricity to the injured area, that predicted its success. Since the drugs weren't working, I didn't have anything to lose.

The test session went really well. I vibrated from the waist down and noticed that much of the pain in my hips and legs was gone. After taking my first few steps without crutches in years, I was sold.

Oprah Calling

In the midst of all this, out of nowhere, Oprah Winfrey's people called. They were shooting a show on survivors, and they wanted to fly a crew out to interview me for it. At this point, I didn't care at all about more publicity, but Teresa loved Oprah and told me I had to do it. More as a favor to her than anything else, I agreed to the interview.

It went well enough for them to fly me to Chicago and be on the show. The first segment featured a reality tv star talking about surviving under extreme situations.

This was followed by a segment on two kids who had been struck by lightning, and one with someone who had been buried in a car in an avalanche. Then, somewhere around the time the reality star was going to parachute down on to the stage in a stunt, I'd get my turn.

When it came, the first thing I thought about was how really, really good Oprah is at what she does. I wasn't nervous at all and, before I could really think about it, was talking about the Chinese guy and the lights that I saw leaving people's bodies.

When she asked me what I thought it meant, I told her that I believed that the way you lived your life was important, because it determined how you left it. We were running out of time, but Oprah told everyone to hold on and that we were going to keep the cameras on.

At some point during the extended discussion, I became proactive and started asking the survivors to compare notes. By the time we were through, Oprah seemed really excited, came up to thank me, and left to go to her dressing room.

Thinking we were done, I went back to mine, which was in the opposite direction, located right near the stage door, a full city block away from hers. As we got ready to leave, I saw Teresa turn around, her eyes wide as saucers.

From her reaction, I figured she was looking at Oprah. But I wasn't expecting Oprah, now in an orange velour track suit, to come up, tap me on the shoulder, grab me by the arm, and tell me that was the best interview she had ever done in 25 years of broadcasting.

I figured she was just being polite, but there was a note waiting at the hotel asking me to be on her radio show with a bunch of spiritualists. I was kind of a flop that night and barely paid attention to what the guests were saying. I felt a lot better when that month's edition of O Magazine came out. There I was, on the inside of the back cover, talking about the brightness of one's life.

Coming clean – Sort of

After Oprah, I thought I was a rock star again. I was invincible. First I had a shoulder operation. Then, in June of 2007 I had my implant, which was really just a software package and battery pack inserted just above my right hip in the love-handle area of my lower back.

A wire ran internally up to my spine where 16 contact points had been imbedded, and a remote control device let me adjust the amount of electricity and vibration. I don't think anyone, including the experts, knew why this worked, but it did. That was all I cared about.

Next I told the doctors I wanted to get off methadone. When it was first prescribed to me, they truly thought that I, like most everyone else on it, would be on it for life. But I hated the drug to the point I was willing to risk the withdrawal.

The doctors were not encouraging. Methadone stays in the system at least three times longer than the other opiates including heroin. The withdrawal, they warned me, would be extremely painful and, due to methadone's extended half-life, would take months. Turns out they were telling the truth. Quitting methadone was the single most difficult thing I have ever encountered.

We started by reducing the dosage very gradually, a gram at a time. Each gram was like having my soul pulled out, but at a painfully slow speed. It didn't seem like it was working, so I thought about going cold turkey. When I flew up to Seattle to visit Cholly and forgot my methadone, I figured, "Fuck it. He has some vicodin so I might as well do it now."

Cold turkey took an entire month, in which horrible hallucinations, insomnia, and catatonia were the rule, not the exception. But by 2008, my head started to clear -- just in time for the recession.

We were stuck with a big mortgage and in bad shape financially. Because it was so beautiful, it sold quickly, enabling us to get out of debt and into the new American rite of passage: downsizing.

Fortunately, I'd recovered enough from the surgical procedures to go back in the gym. But the stimulator controlled only about 40% of the pain, so Dr. Audell had reintroduced opiates in low doses.
Aware of the danger, I was worried about becoming addicted to opiates again. Not that it stopped me from combining the opiates with Somas. Thinking I could control my drug intake, I felt myself becoming stronger, clearer, and ready to face the real world.

My timing wasn't ideal. The music industry was in free-fall, so it took a few years to get work. And that didn't happen until I reconnected with my old friend, Cyndi Lauper.

She was riding a very successful comeback, due largely to her wise decision to end an extended hiatus by opening for Cher in the first of her farewell tours. That way, she played larger venues to receptive audiences, rather than headline smaller theaters.
She followed that with a Grammy for the album, *Memphis Soul*. When I called to congratulate her, she told me she was in a quandary, because they couldn't come up with a way to film it. Thinking I had found my ticket back, I promised to think about it.

I knew this could be my ticket back, but although the pain was better than it had been, it was still worse than I had let on. To combat it, I was secretly taking more than the prescribed dosages of the pain medications.

Thinking I could stave off the addictions and still maintain a professional work ethic, I decided to go down to Tijuana, pick up a stash of pills, and take them only when necessary. So I called up my longtime production manager and set up the trip. It was the worst decision of my life.

PART THREE

Redemption Song

Burning Bridges

I spent a lifetime burning bridges.
Older now, I stand on ridges,
Pondering how to get across
And of graces squandered, opportunities lost.
The chasms beckon, my soul benign,
The fall far steeper than the climb.

Tijuana Bound

It was one of those great fall mornings we sometimes get in Los Angeles. Cool temperatures, and not a cloud in the sky. I got up early as usual, but instead of going to the gym, I was on my way to San Diego with my friend and production manager, Dave Daniels.

Officially I was tagging along so he could use the carpool lane and get to a meeting with his attorney on time. Along the way, I told Nancy, we'd iron out some ideas about the Cyndi Lauper project.

As with all good lies, there was an element of truth to both excuses. The carpool lane did cut an hour off the drive, and he was only available for the prep, not the shoot itself. So as true as those reasons were, they were not the real reason and not even the real destination.

Stopping only to hit the bathroom and refill our coffee cups, we hit the border as planned, at 11:30. That gave us plenty of time to find a doctor, get a prescription for SOMAs, and be back in the U.S.A. before rush hour.

We crossed the border without problems, parked, and walked across the bridge to downtown Tijuana. I wasn't crazy about walking, which was painful and difficult for me, but Dave thought it was safer than driving around Tijuana.

I wasn't sure that walking around was any better. Along the way, we walked past a policeman. Although small in stature, he was a policeman nonetheless. I remember waving to him as we walked by.

Luckily, we quickly found a doctor, with the improbable name of Carlos Castaneda. Rather than mystical advice, he agreed to write us prescriptions for Somas.

Next I asked him if he could give me 500. That's a lot of pills, so I was expecting the raised eyebrow he gave me. But I showed him all my paperwork, described how difficult the trip down to Mexico was on me, and promised that every single one of the pills were for me.

Finally he relented, and, with prescriptions in hand, we walked a couple of blocks to a street lined with pharmacies just off Tijuana's main drag. The first few we hit only had Mexican-manufactured SOMAs. Wary of the fillers they used, we kept asking until at last, we found a pharmacy that stocked American-made pills.

Oddly, at no point did anyone in the pharmacy ask us for a prescription. It was so casual that I remember thinking the prescriptions were merely a formality to get us back across the border, With my pills in hand, we walked across the bridge to our car.

At some point, Dave told me that the woman in the pharmacy had gotten a phone call asking if there were Americans there. Before I could even process that thought, a group of police, led by that same cop I had smiled at, surrounded us. And there I was, holding a giant bag of pills in my hand.

Dave, who had sensibly stuffed the pills down his

pants, fared better. Luckily, the Mexican police are, I found out later, extremely homophobic and only perform a cursory body search on men. As a result, they never found his pills.

I didn't get off as easy. Waving the pills they took from me, they acted like they'd just caught Mexico's most wanted drug lord. Then we were manhandled, cuffed and thrown in the back of a police car with another young American, who looked like he was badly in need of a fix, and taken to a small police station bordering downtown Tijuana.

Foolishly, I still didn't think we had broken any laws and still thought we could buy our way out of all of this with $100. But once the cops pulled me out of the cell and began to question me, I started to understand that we were in big trouble.

First they wanted to know the name of the pharmacist who had sold us the pills. I told them I couldn't remember the name or the location of the store, which was the truth.

Without saying a word, they threw me into the back of a police car and drove me back to the exact street where we bought the pills. It was obvious that they had known where we had bought the pills and who we had bought them from.

The extent of the setup was confirmed when they pulled a group of people out of the pharmacy, including the man and woman who had sold us the pills. Even though I was pretty sure I knew who they were, I said I couldn't identify any of them with any sort of confidence.

It didn't matter. They pulled the pharmacist and his female assistant out of the lineup, threw them into a police car, and drove all of us back to the jail.

When we got back, they handcuffed us to the cell doors for what seemed like hours. Finally two cars pulled up, and the pharmacist, Dave, the junkie, the pharmacist's assistant and I were driven to the Federal building.

Dave and the junkie went to a quick release center, while the three of us were escorted into the Federal building, where we were told we could be held for 72 hours while the D.A. decided whether to press charges, set bail, or let us go.

After being processed, I was thrown into a bug-infested holding cell with ten other guys. The cell had one bunk with two berths, (so my bed was the concrete floor and a dirty blanket). There was also a porcelain toilet with no seat in one corner of the cell.

By the time they brought me downstairs to the D.A's office the next morning, I was a mess. I hadn't slept. I was scared. I was starving, and I was filthy.

Feeling at the end of my rope, I was relieved and surprised when the two district attorneys were accommodating and nice. Also nice but completely ineffectual were two men from the American consulate. You'd think from all the movies that they'd be dashing and helpful, but they were grim, humorless, and powerless to do more than hand me a booklet that explained my rights -- or lack of them -- in the Mexican injustice system.

Ray of Light

They also warned me that the prisons in Mexico were shockingly different from the ones we have in the U.S. Unlike the U.S. and most other civilized countries, the Mexican system considers you guilty until proven innocent, not innocent until proven guilty. It is a critical distinction.

Given the amount of pills I had on me, they predicted I'd be transferred to prison for the attempted distribution of 500 *pastillas* (pills). And, saving the worst for last, they had talked to my wife, explained the situation, suggested she start putting together money for a legal defense fund, and told her I'd call her later in the morning.

Overcome with shame, I turned to the list of available criminal attorneys in the booklet they had left. I picked one, Carlos Garcia, primarily because he spoke English. The D.A. then gave me a brown manila envelope with my personal effects, including my cell phone. They told me I could make two phone calls on it before they took it back.

I immediately called Nancy, who was in shock but was relieved I was alive. She told me she understood the severity of the situation and that Dave, who supposedly had been released the night before, was still missing. (He turned up eventually.) I asked her to call various friends who might be able to help and, with the clock ticking, said goodbye.

I don't think I've ever felt as bad in my life, knowing what I was putting her and the rest of my family through. They didn't deserve this, and I didn't deserve them. I didn't even deserve to live.

Before despair took over, I forced myself to dial Carlos Garcia, who said he would be right over. Placing the cellphone in the envelope, I handed it to the authorities and was escorted back to the filthy cell.

The lawyer came within a few hours, but those hours seemed like forever. I was surprised at how young he was, and how good looking. More importantly, I was surprised by the light he generated. I hadn't seen that in anyone since I got to Mexico.

Deciding to trust my instincts, I believed him when he said he would find the doctor I had gone to, have my medical records translated into Spanish, and hit the judge with everything he could.
"You'll get out," he said, "IF the judge reads our side of the story."

New Kid on the Block

Although my mind was reeling at this point, I had enough presence of mind to not show any weakness in front of the serious dudes in the cell. Rather than cower, I approached the most formidable, a gangbanger named Angel, who was tattooed head to toe with gang and prison tattoos.

While he was practicing Muay Thai, with a bravado I didn't feel, I approached him and demonstrated some Jiu Jitsu moves. I also showed him my defensive moves of Hwa Hrang Do. It is a Korean martial art, based on Japanese Jiu Jitsu, that I had studied. I don't know whether he was intrigued or just surprised, but the gesture seemed to gain the respect of a bona fide *hombre malo* (bad guy).

My next demonstration of machismo came when a prisoner tried to take my blanket away from me. Rather than give up one of my last worldly possessions, I resisted and threw him down on his knees. That seemed to satisfy the others, who didn't bother me after that.

The next day, I was taken out of the cell for another round of interrogation. The police tried once again to get me to admit that the two pharmacists were the ones who sold me the *pastillas*.

I was still pretty sure they were and was also pretty sure that the police knew all along who they were. I wondered if they were all in collusion, and that they would force me to buy my way out of prison. So, again sticking with my instincts, I refused to identify them.

Even without my testimony, they arrested the man and the woman. The woman ended up in the cell next to us, where she cried for three straight days. The man was in my cell. He assured me that he wasn't involved, but the more I talked to him, the less I believed him.

Around three in the afternoon of that third day, they took the pharmacists out for one more round of questioning. In the depths of my depression, I realized I was alone in the cell for the first time. Thinking I had about 30 minutes of solitude, I tied my T-shirt to the metal bunk bed and tried to choke myself to death. I managed to pass out twice, but each time, the T-shirt loosened and I'd find myself still very much alive.

When the pharmacist came back, he told me that he was being released, solely because I hadn't positively identified him. He said this was lucky for both of us, because if I had identified him, he would have had to become a witness against me. Rather than comment, I started to choke myself for the third time.

Immediately understanding what was happening, he stopped me and explained that the guards would put me in full restraints, including a straight jacket, if they found out I was trying to kill myself. I told him that I'd rather be dead than go to prison and asked him to hold the knot tight until I died. Of course he refused.

The police then came and got me for one last round of questioning. Two plainclothes officers brought me into a small room and pushed me onto a metal chair. There was no table, no spotlights, just that chair. They cuffed my hands and feet to it and began to question me about the pharmacists.

It was classic good cop, bad cop, straight out of the movies. The larger one bellowed threats, ranting, raving, and threatening to beat me up. All the while, the smaller one pretended to be trying to calm his partner down.

I kept repeating that I wasn't sure that they were the two I had bought the pills from. The "bad" cop began to vigorously shake me as he screamed at me, while the "good" cop screamed at him.

Since I wouldn't change my answers, they told me it would go a lot easier for me if I gave the two up, regardless of whether or not I recognized them. They handed me a long statement prepared in Spanish and told me to sign it, but I told them I wasn't going to sign anything I couldn't understand.

The "good" cop told me I was making a mistake, because my signature was the only way he was going to be able to control the "bad" cop. When I continued to refuse, the "bad" cop pulled out a big plastic bag and took off his belt. I knew that I wouldn't be able to withstand a beating, but I still wouldn't sign.

But instead of beating me, they loosely put the belt around my neck. Without really registering what they were about to do, I still wouldn't tell them what they wanted to hear. After my third or fourth denial, they slipped a plastic bag over my head and tightened the belt around the bottom of it so I couldn't breathe.

After the initial shock of feeling the belt tighten and the air go out of the bag, the absurdity of the situation hit me. Just minutes before, I had tried unsuccessfully to strangle myself, and now these bozos were trying to suffocate me with some low-rent waterboarding. Seizing the moment, I happily sucked as much of the plastic bag down my throat. As I started gagging and convulsing, I crossed my fingers that these guys would kill me.

But all they did was watch me pass out. After several times taking the bag on and off, the "good" cop realized I wasn't going to break. After a few more minutes, they gave up and escorted me back to my cell.

When I told the pharmacist what had just happened, he thanked me profusely, almost to the point of tears. He told me they wouldn't have beaten me or done anything that left marks, for fear of getting in trouble with the human rights activists who periodically showed up in the prisons under a humanitarian flag.

More to the point, he also hinted that the cartels ran the pharmacies and had paid to get him out. Then he told me that there were negotiations for my own release taking place at the border. I wasn't sure I believed him. Failing to convince him to help me with another suicide attempt, I watched him leave. It was almost ten years to the day of the plane crash.

Jailhouse Rock

Around ten o'clock that night, the authorities rounded up me and the other prison-bound inmates. I was chained and shackled to a group of criminals, in a van with sirens flashing, driving into the Mexican night. I hadn't really slept in three days. Or eaten. Or washed. Or brushed my teeth.

Scared and disoriented, the only thing I could see through the open slit of the van's window was *La Pinta*, the prison, rising out of the slums of Tijuana like a huge monolith, towering over its shanty-like surroundings. The police vehicle sped up, as if being pulled towards its destination. I couldn't stop the fear and anxiety from welling up in my throat.

After being kept waiting in a holding cell, we endured a thorough "strip to your skivvies" search. Next, they pulled some information out of us and led us, handcuffed, hands behind our backs, into an outside corridor of chain-link fencing with large gates, locked with giant "Master Brand" padlocks.

An official stood at each locked gate, with keys to the padlocks. A small dog like Cerberus at the gates of hell turned out to be a giant rat, welcoming us to prison.

Next we were led to yet another holding area. Safely ensconced behind two-inch plexiglass windows, were lawyers, prison officials, and *actuarias* (court secretaries).

After meeting with the appropriate official, I was left with the others in the cold night air for a few hours before heading into a small room. There we underwent a lengthy process of form filling and fingerprinting. Although computers were everywhere, this was done the old-fashioned, slow way by hand.

In a stroke of good luck, I noticed that a small, barred window next to the fingerprinting room had smoke billowing out. Juan, a portly, English speaking guy in my group, explained that this cell block was reserved for the *los viejos*, who were at least 60 years old. Since they enjoyed slightly better living conditions than the rest of the inmates. I immediately set my sights on that cellblock. Just having that goal brought my spirits up a little.

After they finally took my fingerprints, I was escorted to the most infernal place I'd ever been in my life, *Ochito*, or Little Eight. Inmates are "only" supposed to be there for 72 hours, but since Carlos had filed an appeal as a delaying tactic, I ended up spending almost eight days there.

Behind the Eight Ball

The first thing I noticed when I got inside *Ochito* was graffiti, profanity, gang symbols, lovers' notes, and dates, that completely covered floor, walls and ceilings, scratched or written with pens or pieces of metal that had somehow been smuggled into the cell.

Then I noticed the bugs. Mostly these were *chi-chi's* (bed bugs with a vicious bite) and huge roaches. They covered the walls so thoroughly that the concrete seemed to be a breathing organism. Worse were the rats, who ran rampant and fearlessly, especially at night.

The "bathroom" was equally repulsive. The toilet was a hole that doesn't flush but goes directly into a sewer. There was no sink, just a spigot of the garden type, coming out of the wall. A three-foot cinder block partition separated the bathroom from the beds, but it did nothing to stem the pervasive stink of vomit, excrement and urine.

Surprisingly, despite everyone there being in lockdown, the prison was also noisy and in constant flux. Prisoners came and went throughout the night or were transferred in and out of the general population, so the place was hopping every night from eight or so until two in the morning.

That meant the actual number of inmates vacillated from 18 to 34 men, all crammed into a cell that had been designed for three prisoners. Because there were many more men than bunks, most had to sleep on the floor, which became a writhing mess of bodies that tossed and turned throughout the night like undulating water, futilely trying to get comfortable in the filthy, worn blankets and the cold and wet concrete floor.

On this particular evening, I was the 29th person to be crammed into the cell. There were six bunks. Each bunk had two men, sleeping head to feet, in it. That left 17 of us on the floor, wherever there was space. Because I wasn't moving well and in obvious pain, *Huero* (slang for White Boy), the guy who was running the cell because he'd been there the longest, put me in a ground bunk.

It didn't take long to understand that Huero was in control of the cell. By his decree, regardless of the time they arrived, every new inmate was forced to take a cold water bucket bath. Since everyone had been held for at least 48 hours in a filthy hole before they got here, it was a great rule.

That didn't make the freezing water any less a shock to my system. Even worse was having to put the filthy clothes I was arrested in back on. But I didn't have a choice; they were the only things I owned.

With nothing left to do, I lay down on the metal bunk. There was no mattress, just a flimsy, filthy blanket for a cushion and a cover. And a bunkmate, named Pelon.

Pelon was a surly, tattooed gangbanger who definitely did not want to share his bed. Despite sleeping rather soundly (head to foot, mercifully), he tried pushing me off the bunk several times. Because I was unable to sleep, I held my ground and refused to be pushed off the bed.

The flickering hall lights were the only light source in the cell. They never went off, so you couldn't really gauge the passing of time. The only way I knew I had made it through the night was by the brightened windows across the hall and the sounds of a day worker bringing food to someone.

Money for Nothing...

We pretty much wasted the allotted 48 hours trying to decide how to proceed, principally because my attorneys and my family couldn't agree on a game plan. According to my attorney, who was the only person I had direct personal contact with, my American friends wanted to hire an important U.S. attorney to "go down there and scare the daylights out of those

Mexicans." In addition, they wanted to pay off the local Tijuana authorities, who were backed by the cartels, and get me released.

As much as that made sense north of the border, Carlos explained that Mexicans think Americans are burdened with an acute sense of self-importance. As a result, they strategically underestimate the levels of contempt and resentment the local authorities have for *El Otro Lado*.

Waving a big stick, he continued, would do me more harm than good. As counterintuitive as it sounded to a U.S. citizen, Carlos thought we would do better by taking our chances with the system.

I agreed with Carlos, but my friends thought he was too young and good looking to take seriously. Ignoring his advice that they were wasting their money, they tried to buy my way out.

The bartering took place in a little restaurant on the US side of the border with an assortment of my friends, one of whom had $30,000 of his cash on him, and representatives of the Tijuana police.

The Mexicans started the bidding at $3,000. As soon as my friends agreed, the price rapidly jumped to $15, $25, and $50,000. At that point, knowing the price was going to escalate, my friends told the Mexicans they needed more time to get their hands on that kind of money.

I only found out about this when Carlos came to the

prison and told me that my friends weren't listening to him. I wrote a note for Carlos to pass on to them, begging them to stop the negotiations and support Carlos. They agreed, and gave him $5,000, which allowed him to formally represent me. (By law, he couldn't legally represent me until money had changed hands. Up until then, he had been representing me in good faith.)

The episode brought home my isolation. I could have avoided the problem if I had talked to my friends directly, but you only get to use the phone one evening a week. Unless you got to prison with an activated phone card when you were arrested (I didn't), you were limited to making collect calls, which cell phones don't accept. And after years of speed dial, I couldn't pull up a single landline number from memory. I was, in every sense of the word, cut off from the rest of my world.

By the time 72 hours in Ochito was up, we didn't have much to show for our efforts, so Carlos got me a three-day extension. He officially claimed that he needed more time to prepare, but it was more a delaying tactic, designed at keeping me out of prison for as long as possible.

A few days later, I managed to remember my old friend Kevin Wall's number. I already was at the mercy of the Mexican authorities, so, other than insisting he tell the others to let Carlos call the shots, I told him the truth: There was really nothing he could do to help me.

By then, the monotony and the filth were starting to

unnerve me. Because no one was supposed to stay there for more than three days, no one cared about the surroundings. Even if they did, there were no cleaning supplies available. So the only time the cells got cleaned was when the sewer backed up and spewed two inches of sludge onto the floor and into the hallway.

That happened several times that week. When it did, you had to stand in mid-calf waste with giant turds floating around. Then the cleaning crew, who stayed in the hall and never entered the cell, pushed any sewage in the hall back into the cell. Then they passed a broom and some cleaning disinfectant through the bars, and watched as each prisoner got his chance to clean the cell floor.

As he did, everyone else huddled on the bunk with his blankets and personal possessions. By the end, the floor smelled more like disinfectant than bodily fluids. But that, really, was small consolation for the subhuman treatment and violation of basic human rights that were part of daily life.

In this kind of atmosphere, it was not surprising how little personal grooming mattered. Without access to a razor and a mirror or money to pay someone to shave you, it was easier to just stop shaving.

Dental hygiene posed a bigger problem. Without access to a toothbrush or floss, all I could do was rinse my mouth and then use my fingers to try and clean my teeth. (If you're tempted to try it at home, don't bother. It doesn't work.)

In the Midnight Hour

Every once in a while, even in there, you got glimpses of the human spirit. One of these moments happened when Huero told an inmate to sing something.

The inmate captured everyone's attention with a beautiful Mexican song. After he finished, the cell launched an impromptu singing contest, with each person crooning a different number. During a lull, Huero looked at me, grinned, and said it was my turn.

Feeling very much on the spot, I broke into a folk song, "La Aurora," which was one of the few Mexican tunes I knew. I got a smattering of applause, but Huero turned to me, shook his head, and said, "No, no, no. American rock and roll."

Without any hesitation, I broke out into "Rebel Yell" and sung it at the highest decibel level possible. It was my private tribute to Nancy, because it begins with the line "last night my little dancer." Nancy had been competing in dance contests recently with a professional choreographer, so the song reminded me of her.

It went over so well that I did an encore, my version of "Yesterday," which also struck a chord with the "audience." It was the first time in days that I actually enjoyed myself and was also the first good night's sleep I had in a week.

Glory Be's

Around then, I also noticed that everyone, regardless of their crimes or their innocence or guilt, seemed to have found religion in prison. Although prisoners everywhere, stripped of everything including hope, often turn to faith to keep sane, our salvation was due in large part to a remarkable, venerated woman named Sister Antonio.

She and two other nuns, came to the prison with religious icons, reading materials, and candies. Although she used to have free access to the prison, a riot several years earlier restricted her visits to the new arrivals and those who were near death.

The only nice thing in this monstrosity, she would appear like a rose that blooms in winter. Even the most frightening inmates lined up to take some of her offerings. [To find out more about her, Google Sister Antonio of the Tijuana prisons.]

At first I passed over the icons but did take several *Reader's Digests* in English and a handful of faux M&Ms. Given my circumstances, they were extraordinary gifts.

A few days later, I took a Rosary from her. That was a huge step for me, because I had been a devout Catholic, going to mass every day for years. But distrustful of organized religion, which I felt had become corrupt, I had left the Catholic Church some years before. So while I was raised Catholic, I hadn't been to church, received communion or said prayers since the mid-1990s.

In the 20 years before that, however, I usually went to church every day but Saturday. I started going, oddly enough, early one morning after a night tripping on acid. As I was getting home from a wild time, I bumped into my father, who was on his way to church. He asked me what I was doing, and I was so flustered that I changed the subject by asking him why he went to church religiously.

Surprising me, he told me in that totally reasonable voice of his that church was a quiet place where he could put his thoughts and his day together. Without a convincing excuse not to, I went along with him. When I got there, his answer made sense, and I started going too.

Twelve years later, Penny and my contentious divorce was finally settled, and I wanted to remarry. But if divorce is merely frowned upon, remarriage is a sin. T'Boo was also a Catholic and wanted a religious ceremony. Not knowing what to do, I explained my dilemma to the parish priest in New York City.

He suggested getting an annulment, which would leave me free to marry. I thought our two children made the lack of consummation difficult to explain away and told him that would be impossible.

He assured me that wouldn't be a problem. The annulment was not a denial of the marriage's existence, but verification that the marriage should never have happened in the first place.

He wasn't even phased when I told him that the split had been quite bitter, and that my ex-wife would never agree to the annulment. Her wishes didn't matter, he said, because the Church's view was the only one that counted.

That worked for me. A year later, after admitting to a lifestyle of youthful excess, including drugs, alcohol, and partying, we got the official okay: T'Boo and I could get married. And so we did, in the chapel of her old high school, in the shadows of my old neighborhood. It was a full-on, messy blowout, but the irony of that seemed lost on the priests.

Then T'Boo and I split up, and I met Nancy. I had remained very involved in the Church throughout this period and even got Nancy, a registered Pagan if ever there was one, to come along.

By late 1994, when we were living in a beautiful Frank Gehry studio loft in Santa Monica, we got engaged. Being a creature of habit, I went to my new pastor and told him I wanted to remarry. Once again, I was told, with another wink, to get an annulment. And once again, after a lot of money and a bit of time, it would be granted.

Maybe because I had been through this once before, it struck me as the height of hypocrisy. After much soul searching, I reluctantly stopped practicing rituals I no longer believed in. I still considered myself a spiritual person, but I thought my lifelong practice of Catholicism, along with all the prayers, rituals and church services, was over.

But in the living hell of *La Pinta*, the Bible readings, prayers, and icons reminded me of the solace I used to find in the rituals and prayers. So I started saying a Rosary every night, ticking off the Our Fathers, Hail Mary's and Glory Be's on my little red plastic Rosary. The theology notwithstanding, the mantra of prayer helped me to concentrate on the positive, rather than the negative thoughts that were dominating my consciousness.

The Food Network

I knew that I needed to eat in order to keep my strength and health, but that was easier said than done. Meals were served twice a day by inmates who had achieved day worker status, who used giant, greasy ladles to spoon out gruel from big open cauldrons into styrofoam cups that passed us through the bars.

The cups were larger than the space between the bars, so half the food ended up on the floor. There were no utensils, so you either used your hands or just tried to drink the slop down.

Breakfast was clumps of what most likely was eggs but more closely resembled vomit, floating in a fatty caldo (soup). Absolutely horrid, especially for a notoriously picky eater who, when little, would never allow the few foods I'd eat touch each other on the plate.

The other meals were no better. Most of the inmates loved the *chilaquiles*, a soggy mess of chips, cheese, and chili beans, and the *chicharones*, soggy pork rinds cooked in some derivative of tomato sauce. They also liked the greasy stews, made with unrecognizable boiled meat, chicken or pork, and, a mealy soy fake meat, cooked in a greasy tomato soup with what may have been potatoes. But the only meal I could really stomach was the chicken and rice, which I would take without the soup.

Sometime between six to nine p.m., they also brought a very sweet tea (served hot) or a sugared milk that's either white or brown (although you'd be hard pressed to taste the chocolate) or pink (faux strawberry), served either hot or cold, with *pan dulce* (a plain roll with sugar lumped on top). Even if I were hungry, I always gave mine to one of the other prisoners. There was never a shortage of takers.

I couldn't keep anything down the first two days, but, sensing myself grow weaker, I forced the vile stuff down my mouth, gagging all the while. The temptation to throw up was intense, but I did everything I could to keep each mouthful down.

Besides not ever really knowing what you were eating, you also never knew when you were going to be fed either. One day, breakfast would come at seven and lunch at two; the next, breakfast would come at nine and lunch at one. It didn't matter since no one was going anywhere anyway, but was one more way the days seemed like weeks.

Out of Time

The delay in getting funds to Carlos, made it

impossible to mount a preemptive defense. We were out of time. At ten o'clock at night on the seventh day of my imprisonment, I was taken to the *locutorio*, a series of glass-plated booths where inmates are summoned to talk to their lawyers, representatives of the court, or prison authorities.

The female officer I talked to wasn't fluent in English but managed to explain that I was going to be processed into the prison.

I was then taken to the last cell on the block to await final processing. Because they were waiting to find out where they were going to do their time, everyone in the cell was on edge, I sat there through the night and morning and into the afternoon, until almost everyone else had been called.

Finally, those of us who were left were taken to the courtyard in front of *Ochito*, where a number of prison employees, mostly women, were assigning cells to the prisoners. When it was my turn, I was told I'd be put into a cell with a lot of Americans.

She had intended it as a favor -- the second act of kindness inside the prison -- but I was horrified. I didn't object to the fact that most of the Americans in there were young junkies. The real reason was that the cells in the general population housed an average of 25 inmates in each 8x13' cell. By comparison, the ones in *Tercero Edad* were almost spacious.

With as much force as I could muster, I told her I was *sesenta anos* (60), had *muchas problems medical*, and *needed* to be in *Tercero Edad.* I'm sure she knew I was begging. In one of the very few breaks I caught since my arrest, she relented.

Sometime, just after midnight, broken emotionally, in serious pain, and filthy, I got the official notice that I was going to be in jail until I went to trial. I had ample warning that this was going to happen, but I still went into a state of shock.

The Gates of Hell

From what I could determine over the next few months, the prison was a seven-building compound that's enclosed by a massive 20-foot concrete wall. Each of these buildings were made of concrete and steel. Two-feet tall windows sat six feet off the ground, and ran the length of each cellblock.

Guards with automatic weapons kept up constant surveillance from a number of watchtowers. The perimeter walls were topped with frightening barbed wire, and the interior yard had been designed around a system of hurricane fences and gates that created three separate, fenced in areas that herded prisoners as if they were farm animals.

A concrete slab functioned as a soccer and exercise field. Small holding pens of 12-foot tall double-gauge hurricane fencing littered the landscape. Banks of 40 or so payphones lined one side of each yard.

There were also several smaller buildings. The administration staff was housed in a small separate building in the very front of the prison. The kitchen and infirmary were also set off, as was a small stand-alone shack by the yard called "The Store."

Day workers ran back and forth from the yards to get products like milk, cereal, soda, juice, yogurt, cookies, chips, candy, toilet paper, soap, razors, toothbrushes, toothpaste, and notebooks. The inmates paid for these with the prison's internal currency, a chit they called *vale*.

The building that housed us *viejos*, the *Tercero Edad* (Third Age) is the largest building in the prison. The inmates lived on the first floor, next to the Intensive Care cells, which is really a hospice since no one seemed to leave there alive. The Red Cross had an office in the building, but they were rarely there.

There was also the AIDS cellblock and a cellblock for all the gay prisoners (including anyone caught having sex with a man in the prison), and the TB ward, located behind the ICU. Then, crammed in somewhere, was the asylum, where the crazies lived. Finally, above us on both sides of the second and third floor were the troublemakers who require extra guards.

Next to that was *Ochito* and the *locutorio* and some fenced in but open areas of concrete, which were used by inmates and their visitors. When an inmate was in this area, he generally was shackled hand and foot. If he wasn't, he had to walk with his hands behind his back, as if he were cuffed. At the first sign of violence, the guards were quick to cuff and shackle him.

The only building I could see from my cell was building number two, a two-story structure directly across from us. The bottom floor was for guards, but also had cells for conjugal visits, which took place on Wednesdays. The top floor was reserved for sexual offenders of all types. Visiting organizations such as the Red Cross set up shop in the courtyard, when it was time for flu shots or other special occasions.

Another building housed all the day workers except for two, Felipe and Hector, who live in my cellblock. These men wore sleeveless blue shirts over their grey prison sweats, and ran to every building all day and throughout the night to tell prisoners they were wanted in the *locutorio*.

Other inmates wearing orange shirts did things like bring the drinking water and the sugar water that they call *jugo* (juice) to the cells. They also brought inedible *tortas* (sandwiches), made of soggy, stale bread, a few bits of carne asada or processed ham, processed cheese and a few bits of wilted lettuce and tomatoes, raw onions (which they throw on everything), and some mayo substitute. For a real treat, there also was some alien version of pizza, which was always delivered stone cold. For no apparent reason, the orange shirts also worked in the infirmary as quasi-nurses.

The kitchen workers wore black aprons and hauled the giant cauldrons of slop on flat wheel carts. These cauldrons were checked for contraband by guards at all the various gates leading to the buildings. Sometimes they stuck their entire arm into the pot. You never let yourself dwell on what ended up in that pot.

These groups of inmates worked 14 to 16 hour days without pay or reduced sentences. They made up for it by becoming dealmakers and charging the inmates *vales* for services rendered.

There were two other buildings in the prison. Building number six was the maximum-security three-story building, with the worst offenders on the top floor. All the prisoners in six were cuffed and shackled whenever they were removed from this building. Building number seven was a three-story women's prison.

There was also a bandshell where they used to have concerts, as well as two small churches. But in the aftermath of the same riot that restricted Sister Antonio's access to prisoners, concerts and church services had been indefinitely suspended.

Little House on the Prairie

Like all the other cellblocks, mine contained seven 8'x13' cells and an eighth cell that was about 8'x24'. That eighth cell was originally a shower and washroom, but it's been a cell for years.

Each cell was jammed with three triple, metal bunk beds and one single bed. Each bed had a seriously strained, bug encrusted, ¾ inch foam mattress and a thin blanket, which was the only thing you got when they locked you up. If, as it happened in *Ochito*, there were more prisoners than beds, you slept and lived on the floor.

A three-foot-high, three-feet wide cinder block wall divided the sleeping/living area from the bathroom. It had a metal toilet, a six-foot tall water spigot and a stainless steel metal sink.

Any thoughts I had of standing under the spigot and taking a real shower were quickly dashed when I found out that the spigot wasn't used for showering. Instead, we used seven buckets, balanced on top of each other in a pyramid.

Since the water is turned on and off at inexplicable and unpredictable times, everyone made sure these buckets were always filled. (When the water is off, the buckets are used to flush waste down the toilet in lieu of actual flushing.) There's never any hot water. By the end of November, the water is always very, very cold.

The toilet sat atop a two-foot tall concrete pedestal with a smaller one-by-one foot concrete step in front of it. There was no toilet seat, just a round metal rim everyone sat on. Although the inmates had hung a makeshift flimsy curtain between the toilet and the sink, there was never any privacy anywhere.

Dr. Hook's Medicine Show

My reluctance to use the toilet, combined with the effects of a dreadful diet, soon got me in real trouble. Since I had been in prison, one of the only people I was allowed to see was the doctor. Ironically, he was the doctor who prescribed the medicine that got me here in the first place, Even more ironically, his name was Dr. Carlos Castaneda.

He had prescribed all sorts of medicine for a variety of ailments, including a wracking, wheezing cough and an alternating case of serious diarrhea and constipation. The condition was caused by my massive opiate intake of the last 10 years, so I knew that without medical relief, the blockage would kill me without medical relief.

To treat the problem, Dr. Castaneda had prescribed laxatives, which I desperately needed, and Ensure, to supplement the inedible frijoles, rice, potatoes or the rubbery, unidentifiable meat we were fed. Par for the course, the supplies never arrived. Reaching my breaking point, I crossed my fingers and entered the bowels, so to speak, of the prison's medical services.

The doctor in charge of the infirmary was an old guy named Dr. Naranja. I had a soft spot for him because he had been an early advocate of my release, going so far to write a letter confirming the pills were for legitimate medical use. It didn't do a bit of good, but it was still more than anyone else had done.

Even so, he hardly inspired confidence. Judging by the people in the infirmary, amputation seemed to be a favorite hobby of his, with neglect a close second. One person entered with a toe infection and came back to the cell minus a leg. A diabetic was ignored until he lost first one leg at the hip and then the other. An 86-year-old man named Poppa, who was one of the prison's original inmates, also lost both legs and subsequently lived in dire fear that he'd someday be released.

More recently, two men from my cell had gotten sick, went to the infirmary, and left in coffins, without anyone knowing exactly why. The inmates were quick to tell me that neither of the men slept in my bed. I wasn't convinced.

At any rate, I didn't feel I had a choice besides going. But when I explained my problem to the nurses, they thought it was one of the funniest things they had ever heard. They were still laughing when, in full view of everyone, they gave me my first public enema.

That cured me of my reluctance to use the bathroom. After being so humiliated, I made it a point to use the toilet once a day. Not that I ever really got used to doing my business in full view of my cellmates, with only a sheer, tattered curtain separating me from the others.

(With this in mind, I was particularly grateful that my teeth were all right, because the dentists were even scarier than the doctors. The chair, X-ray machines and equipment were all straight from the Sixties. None of them worked, because most of their insides had been stripped and sold. Toothaches were treated by extraction, which explained the proliferation of toothless mouths in the cell.)

Grumpy Old Men

A corridor, approximately six feet wide and one hundred feet long, ran the length of the cellblock. In one of the few perks of the retirement wing, the guards opened our cell doors in the morning and didn't close them until the evening, so we could walk that corridor all day. (In the other cells, the prisoners only got to go out of the cell for 90 minutes every week.)

The cellblock door was in front of cell one, and there was a window by the eighth cell where the smokers I had spotted early on hung out. The rest of the corridor was filled with guys playing dominos and checkers, doing their laundry, setting up shop and even selling gaudy and often extremely clever wares, such as hats, bags, and wallets that they made from materials like paper, cardboard and salvaged food wrappers, which were silvered aluminum on one side and colorful on the other.

Like suburban businessmen at the weekly poker game, they complained about the abuses and malfeasance of daily prison life. But they also bragged that with only ten of us in the cell and the ability to "walk the ward," we were much better off than the rest of the prisoners.

The only real downside to this, one they don't mention, was that ours was the only cellblock that didn't segregate prisoners by their crimes. In the rest of the general population, violent criminals were in one building; drug offenders in another; sex criminals in another, et. al. But here the only thing you had in common with the others was making it to 60.

Literally. The reason the our cell was 60 percent roomier than the others had nothing to do with the Mexicans' respect for the elderly. Instead, it was a sobering comment on how few prisoners in the system live that long.

In practical terms, it meant I was locked up with murderers, pedophiles, and, the worst of all, *los locos*. Because, yes, being crazy is also a crime in Mexico. True to their name, *los locos* were unpredictably violent and hence, the ones you most needed watch out for.

The Sting

Relatively speaking, though, certain things were undeniably better. In the federal building, there was no shower or running water. In *Ochito,* there was a cold-water bath with a communal bucket and soap, but no towels or clean clothes. But in *Tercero Edad*, there was this thing called a stinger.

I didn't even know of its existence until Alfredo, the boss of the cell, lent me a bucket that had been heated by one of these things. It was made out of copper wire wrapped about a bit of metal and a clever electric plug made out of bottle caps, tape and bent metal prongs. While it seemed like a sure-fire way to get electrocuted, it brought a full bucket of water, about 20 inches high and 14 inches in diameter, to a decent temperature in about two hours.

You can't imagine what a difference that made. Since my activity level was very low and my cell and clothes relatively clean, I only showered every other day. Otherwise, the detergent and harsh conditions would dry out my skin too much. Even so, being able to use hot water for the bath became one of the few pleasures available in this dump.

You also learned to be inventive about personal grooming. Three guys in the cell rented out little metal nail clippers, which some visitors had smuggled in. Since I didn't have any money, I took my lead from the other inmates, bit my nails, and then filed them on the concrete wall for that rugged, just manicured look.

Laundry was done prison style, as well. To mimic the function of the center-piece in a conventional washer, the inmates cut a soda bottle in half, open side out, and attached it to a broomstick handle. They plunged it up and down until the water turned a dirty brackish grey/ brown.

Most rinsed and wrung the clothes in their buckets, but I had trouble bending over the bucket and used the concrete sink in cell eight instead. Once the clothes were wrung, they were hung on one of three lines that run the length of the cell block. Most of the Mexicans apparently did laundry this way all their lives, but for me, it was very hard work.

Since at least half the inmates were always covered in sores from insect bites, which frequently became infected, I'd thoroughly shake out my blankets and search under the mattress for *chi-chis* (bed bugs) every day. Then, on every third day, I'd completely strip the bed and the thin blanket that passes for a bottom sheet. That sheet, which the only thing between me and the smelly, horribly stained foam mattress, was too precious to wash.

It seemed to work. The guy in the bunk beneath me had a chronic problem with these nasty bloodsuckers, but I was only bitten a few times. I credit my routine of vigilance for that. It was a small victory, but a victory nonetheless.

To Have and Have Not

Just like the outside world, prison was divided into the haves and have-nots. In jail, however, almost everyone entered as a have not, with only the clothes they were wearing when they were arrested. Usually the clothes were filthy and infested with bugs.

If you're lucky, you also got an even filthier, stained, two-inch foam mattress and a well-worn, flimsy blanket. That's the extent of your worldly possessions. Thus, once you're in the cell, you are completely dependent on the kindness of strangers for absolutely everything.

In this regard I was really lucky landing in cell number 127-A1, number 2, which we call cell seven. In the hierarchy of things, we weren't that important. That honor went to the first cell, which more or less ran the entire block.

They designated assignments for washing the hall, assigned cells, and functioned as a liaison between the prison and the prisoners. They also announced the arrival of drinking water, which was poured through the bars from a big plastic container with a funnel made from the top half of a soda bottle into the prisoner's bucket.

They also announced store deliveries and meals, and acted as town criers, walking the block, hawking products. And, when the time came, they collected the prisoners and brought them to the blue shirts.

That first cell was led by a nice guy called, Asael, but we were far away from that action. In addition to being the cleanest cell on the block, I was happy to find out that there were two other English speaking prisoners in there.

To my surprise, the men all greeted me with a surprising kindness. They gave me with some well-worn sweatpants, a sweatshirt, T-shirt, socks and underwear. Everything was a little large, full of holes, and marked with the initials of everyone else who had worn them. I didn't care. They were a lot better than what I had been wearing.

Next, an inmate named Mingus, who soon became my best friend, gave me an almost new toothbrush. I had never really thought a used toothbrush could mean so much, but after days without having one, it was one of the best gifts I've ever received. For the next two weeks I lived in these borrowed clothes, used that old toothbrush, got small handouts of toilet paper, and took chillingly cold bucket baths with a borrowed bucket.

Everybody's in Show Biz

The guys I was living with might as well have come from central casting. Alfredo, for instance, was three years into a ten-year sentence for who knows what. He seemed very well educated and spoke a smattering of English, which he occasionally studied. He was also teaching himself German. Very "Padron" looking, he always looked clean-shaven and showered.

Alfredo had a schedule for everything that went on in the cell, including when the TV is on, what we watch, and when it's lights out. He got a little dictatorial with the rules and didn't seem to think anything was strange about always watching what he wanted, going to sleep when he was tired, and making everyone quiet in the morning until he woke up.

He was the only other inmate in the cellblock other than myself who exercised. He worked out vigorously, spending two hours three times a week doing push-ups, sit-ups, various other bodyweight exercises and, using the water bottles as weights, curls and other types of resistance training. Every Thursday, he also ran 50 laps in the yard.

Eduardo, a man without a language, is the other leader in the cell, in charge of the cleaning. He looked like an aristocrat, lived with a Mexican woman in Santa Monica, and spoke English (and passable Spanish, German, and, of all things, Norwegian). He worked for phone companies all his life, both in the U.S., Norway, and Germany, and didn't really have a native language. Like Alfredo, he never explained why he's incarcerated, leading me to believe his crimes were either very violent or sexual. Like Alfredo, he had no aversion to taking control. Together they did a pretty good job.

One of the Americans, Eugene Mingus, who had given me a toothbrush, turned out to be the son of the jazz great, Charlie Mingus. Somehow he had gotten one of those tiny traveling chess sets that folded into itself so that the pieces were stored inside it, and we'd play chess and talk about music.

The Mexican prisoners made no secret of their dislike for Mingus, who was the only black person in the block. They must have assumed I was racist too, because when they talked about him, they called him a nigger. Without thinking, I head-butted the offender's nose, causing it to bleed. From then on, I heard the mutterings, but I never had to confront their prejudice directly again.

I thought that was because that they respected my prowess. Instead, as I learned later, they avoided me because a fight usually won you a trip to solitary confinement. Since the threat of solitary is enough to keep everyone in line, the inmates saw my aggressiveness as a sign I didn't care what happened to me. Thinking I was *el loco*, they rarely messed with me again.

The other American inmate, Robert McClements, was trapped by Mexico's "guilty until proven innocent" doctrine. That policy has incarcerated thousands of people who really are innocent, at least of the crimes they are accused of but who don't have the resources to acquit themselves .

That certainly was the case with McClements, who lived in San Pedro, California. Three months earlier, he wrecked his car on the Mexican side of the border and had been in limbo ever since.

Granted, the accident was lame on his part -- he was 73 and somewhat addled -- but he told me he was just spaced out and didn't even know where he was when the Federales pulled him out of the car.

His bail was set at 20,000 pesos, which is just under $2000, but since he was estranged from his family and had no one to call, he couldn't raise the bail. When I met him, the Catholic Church had just convinced an elderly woman to give him 150 *vale* a week (approximately $12.00).

It was enough to put him in contact with an estranged daughter, but no one knows how much she would help. So, guilty of very little, he remained a prisoner.

Money Changes Everything

To jump from a have not to a have, all you had to do was get your hands on some *vale*, those little chit like pieces of paper that looked like miniature pesos. Some inmates got their hands on them quickly, but I had to wait a few more weeks for my attorneys to finally be able to funnel me clothing and some *vale*.

(Despite being against the rules, some attorneys sneak cash into an inmate's hands. The inmates trade the cash for *vale* with the day workers, who then sell the real money to prisoners about to be released. Since the prison doesn't convert unused *vale* to real money, the day workers and guards keep themselves as busy as a bank. But Carlos played by the rules. So I had to wait.)

Once I had the money, I got a new blanket, three pair of new sweatpants, two sweatshirts, three pair of underwear, socks, and a towel. It barely compensated for the slew of clothes, books, medicine, towels and other items people had sent me that never made it to my bunk, but it made a big difference in my comfort level.

I washed the clothes they gave me when I got into the cell and left them for the new prisoners. I proudly initialed the new items, marking the drab grey clothes as my own, not someone else's.

Even better, I was finally able to buy food. I had eaten very little in those first three weeks. My diet was awful, my immune system was shot, and I had a racking cough and horrible constipation. Throughout, my doctor and attorney kept telling me that I was being sent cans of Ensure, but like everything else, the laxatives and the medicines never showed up. Now, with access to food like yogurt, milk, bran cereal, and an occasional hit of junk food, my health improved.

On Tuesdays, the day we were free to go into the yard for an hour, I shopped for myself. The other days, day workers would bring things to the cells we could buy. My favorites included a fruit plate with watermelon, honeydew, oranges, and papaya, mixed with granola and cottage cheese, and the carne asada, featuring a decent portion of some type of desiccated meat, beans, and salsa. It wasn't Whole Foods, but at least some nutrients were making their way into my body.

With "money," I could visit the yard's "barber." He was an inmate with a pair of clippers connected to a power outlet some 100 yards away by at least 50 extension cords. To protect against lice, I shaved my face and head at the lowest possible setting. It made me look badass, which was sort of cool.

I also bought a new bowl, which was a bigger deal than it sounds. When I first arrived, Eduardo had given me an ex-prisoner's small, broken, leaking plastic bowl. Along with your plate, glass, and storage unit, it is one of every inmate's most precious possessions. When I first arrived, Eduardo had given me an ex-prisoner's small, broken, leaking plastic bowl. Now that I was "in the money," it was one of the first things I bought.

The shopping spree intensified at Mario's. He was the cellblock handyman and made tools, which he sold, out of anything.

It was a true talent. He could break apart discarded razors, strip out the small thin blade, re-sharpen it on the concrete, and end up with a cutting instrument that could shred used bed sheets into strands of thread. He transformed tiny wires from the clothesline and anywhere else he could find them into ingenious needles and hooks. And he could make a stringer. With it, I was finally able to wash my clothes or take a bucket shower with hot water without having to borrow anyone's.

He also made me a pillow out of old pieces of foam mattress, which he stuffed inside a pillowcase of his own making. I even got a separate pillowcase that could be removed and washed in Pine Sol and boiling water. It was a big step up from a pair of sweatpants stuffed into a sheet I had been using, at the expense of my shoulders and spine.

Next, Mario enclosed my bunk with curtains of thin

blue material hung from string fashioned out of thin strips of cloth that he wound and stretched. It didn't block everything out -- I was still in a 13x8 foot cell with nine other men -- but it somehow functioned as a "do not disturb" sign to everyone but the authorities.

Each of these items cost me 60 vale, or about $2.50. As a bonus, Mario spoke excellent English, so the experience was a lot easier. When I complimented him on his command of the language, he told me he had served time in Wichita Falls, Texas. He didn't explain why, but I had a good idea why. In addition to being extremely clever, he was also a murderer.

Another cellmate, Felipe Lucatero, bought me a slightly used, sectioned Tupperware bowl with a plastic *cuchara* (spoon) and lid that he had found in another cell when he was a day worker.

By then, with the idea of this book in my head, I had become addicted to writing things down, which I'd do standing up. One day, he asked me if the rumors about my book were true. Like many of the prisoners, he was encouraging, because he wanted the injustices and inhumanity of their prison lives exposed. He asked me to write of him kindly as my friend.

It's easy to do because in there, he was a friend. Every morning, he and I shook out our blankets in the hall. Since everyone else did it alone, they usually hooted, whistled and teased us. But the ribbing was good-natured and, I flattered myself, tinged with jealousy.

As friendly as I got with him, however, I never forgot

that self-preservation was the rule and that anyone would take advantage of me if it benefited them. So I learned to be wary of even the closest of friends in there. That's just the way it was.

Still, perhaps because of our age or the relative lack of crowding, we appreciated the effects of a combined effort. That's probably why we had the cleanest cell in the entire prison. (Clean being a relative term, since it never got cleaner than the nastiest toilet you could imagine.) To keep it livable, we were the only cell to do a thorough cleaning (called *la talacha*) every day. We rotated the chore, so once a week or so, you got your chance.

The routine began in the bathroom, where you filled the water buckets with all-purpose detergent, which is bought from the prison store. Then you dipped a well-worn brush into the soapy bucket and scrubbed the toilet and the sink. Next you rinsed everything with a gallon milk container that's been converted into a kind of pitcher. Then you used the brush to clean the bathroom floor.

To clean the rest of the cell floor, which was littered each morning with rat droppings, we used a really good sturdy broom with stiff red bristles. We had to sweep everything into a plastic bag liner. Since it was the only one we could get, we had to keep rewashing and reusing it, which was even more disgusting than it sounds.
 Next, everyone piled their personal belongings onto the top of the bed. Using the same dirty water, we washed the cell floor. Then we swept and dried the

floor with one of two blue shammies, which we wrung out and dried until the floor itself was somewhat dry.

Sundays were devoted to *Todos Talacha*, or full cleaning. Then we removed everything from beneath the bunks and cleaned that space too. Since the rats drag their food underneath the bunks to eat, we should probably have done it daily, But the chore was disgusting, and no one really wants to do it.

Once I got money, I was able to buy my way out of the work without losing face. I hired a new "have not," Louis Pardo, to do my share of *la talacha* (ten *vale*) and laundry (five). I felt a bit guilty about it, but at least he now had money to buy toilet paper, soap, and cigarettes. I would normally have objected to helping his smoking habit, but the threat of lung cancer was the least of his problems.

Cigarettes weren't all that were for sale. You could buy drugs, weapons, and shoelaces. Anything was available, as long as you had the money to pay for it.

The guards were the principal source of contraband, particularly narcotics. Given the conditions and the availability, I understood why so many prisoners got hooked. Drugs were way better than the reality of this place.
Just not for me. Once the guards knew I had money, they began hanging around me, tacitly offering me an opportunity to buy their wares. Despite the temptation, I knew that my life was in danger every minute I was in prison. So for one of the first times in my life, I decided to stay sober and be on top of my defensive game.

It was surprisingly easy to just say no. The comforts I could buy -- hot bucket baths, a bit of privacy, better food, toilet paper -- helped a little. But not enough to change the fact that I was all alone, without rights, in a brutal prison environment, at the mercy of some very, very bad people. Drugs had gotten me in here, but they weren't going to help get me out.

Shelter from the Storm

The more the inmates got used to me, they more they'd open up. They'd tell me random things, which I would write down standing up at my bunk. Since it was the middle bunk, it was the perfect height at which to stand and write.

Or so I thought. But it visibly pissed off the guy below me, whom I disliked. I had heard he was a pedophile and defrocked priest. All I knew was that he spent all day copying passages out of the Bible and all night farting.

One day, Felipe, who remained my most ardent literary champion, told me he was serving time for two different crimes. He was guilty of the first, which he didn't describe. But, the second time, he swore on his Bible, which he read daily, the police framed him. Guilty or not, he got an 18-year sentence.
His was a common complaint. The inmates all talked about trumped-up charges and bogus evidence planted by the police to make their cases stronger. Even my lawyers swore it was common practice, especially in Tijuana. *Gobierno malo* (bad government) is the term they all use. I just call it the injustice

system.

The Bible, incidentally, was easily the most popular book in the cellblock. Like the guy in the bunk underneath me, many inmates poured over it all day long, copying passages in notebooks, jotting musings, and trying to push their insights onto anyone who'd listen.

When these zealots saw me reading, they wanted to know why I wasn't reading the Bible, which they claimed was the only way to a better life. I usually told them the truth, which was that I was raised in a strict Catholic environment and was constantly wrestling with and redefining my spirituality.

I had to admit that the traditional Catholic prayers did calm and rejuvenate me. To relax my mind at night and help me cope with the morning, I recited the rosary, complete with dedications for myself, my loved ones, my cellmates, and other unfortunates.

I refrained from adding that I had become addicted to the rituals, repeating them not just in the morning and evening, but also in the afternoon, when I walked the ward. It helped keep the darkness at bay, and added the balance and strength required to resist the evils of this place. I didn't know if I'd ever be a card-carrying Catholic again, but I can tell you this: There's nothing like the power of prayer to help you through a dark and lonely night.

There's a Riot Goin' On

Another day, Alfredo told me all about the riot of 2008. His version, which was less bland, more believable, and far more frightening than the official version of the events, gave me new reasons to be afraid.

The only thing the two versions shared was that the riot started around noon on Sunday, September 16, 2008, and ended 15 hours later, at three in the morning. It flared up again at noon on the 17th for another 12 hours.

Anything beyond that was pretty much up for grabs. It began, as far as I could tell, when *El Comandante*, the commander of the prison, and a guard seized a smuggled cell phone from an inmate on a visiting day and, in full view of a group of other inmates, beat him to death as a punishment.

To retaliate, the inmates broke out of the buildings, spilled out into the open areas, and destroyed the library, the church, and everything they could get their hands on.

Next they lit a bonfire (right in front of my current cellblock) and tossed five inmates, all of whom had collaborated with the guards, into the bonfire, burning them to death. One of these inmates, who tried to escape by dressing as a priest, was burned in his costume. But, Alberto swears, no guards were killed.

In the meantime, the different prison gangs, including the *Paises El Surenos* (the southerners) and *Diez y*

Ocho(18 gang), banded together in the yard. Putting aside their differences, they fought side by side and, building by building, forced all the prisoners out into the yard.

The visitors who had been trapped inside the prison and the captured guards became human shields against the police, who were shooting at them from helicopters.

Like many others, Alfredo didn't want to leave the cell, but the gangs told him he'd be burned alive if he didn't. So he and the others stepped over dead inmates and entered the chaos of tear gas and flying bullets, hiding where they could. As he hunkered down somewhere between the burning churches, he saw clusters of visitors, mostly women and children, trying to hide amidst the burning corpses littering the ground.

As this was going on, a handful of inmates broke into the kitchen, armed themselves with knives and cleaver, and then found their way to the infirmary, where they stole all the drugs.

Around nine o'clock that night, the guards stormed the courtyard, rescuing most of the visitors. Then, sometime after midnight, government security services entered the prison and started shooting indiscriminately.

Most of the inmates by then had found hiding places and were only interested in holding out until daylight and the restoration of order. But not everyone got lucky. Throughout the night, Alfredo, who had taken shelter in a nearby building, heard the screams of inmates caught by the guards. Everyone knew exactly what those screams meant.

The next morning, the trouble started in the women's prison (building seven). Somehow they managed to overpower the guards, steal the keys, and get building six open.

This time, the police retaliated immediately. Using automatic weapons, they shot indiscriminately into the crowd, killing, according to the inmates' estimates, 225 people. Then they loaded the dead bodies into buses and, as if they were alive, propped them up and drove them out of the prison, ostensibly to a mass grave.

Another massacre may have taken place on the wrong side of a hole in the prison wall. A number of inmates used a tunnel underneath the prison to escape. But the police knew about it, and mowed them down as fast as they poured out of the hole.

There were also riots outside the compound, sparked by families of the prisoners. Cars were burned; windows were broken; and at least a few people were shot by police.
To add insult to injury, like a bad riff on the "what happens in Vegas" slogan, whatever happened in the prison stayed in the prison. The media never covered the riot, and relatives, who tried repeatedly to locate their loved ones, were only told that the inmates had been transferred to undisclosed locations. They never were heard of again.
As a result, to this day no one knows how many people

were killed. All they knew was that it took three days to restore order and get the prisoners back in their original cells.

Then the changes started to happen. First the prison underwent an extensive renovation. The old, rusted, bug-infested beds were replaced. This wasn't a concession to the inmates' comfort. As the authorities found out, rusted beds are easily broken and repurposed to pry open bars, locks, and cell doors. Or sharpened to become clubs, shivs and battering rams. Needless to say, no more rusted beds.

Then they set about turning the prison into a modern Gestapo. Suicides, murders, and all sorts of abuse became the order of the day, and what few rights the prisoners used to enjoy were suspended as punishment for rioting.

Before the riots, for example, the inmates had use of the outside areas. There had actually been a bar and easy access to drugs, alcohol, even prostitutes. For those with other inclinations, there was ample time to exercise, go to the library, or spend time in church. They lost those privileges after the riots.

To control the inmates, restrictive fencing that channeled the inmates into specific areas was constructed. The cell doors and locks were strengthened. And prisoners were only allowed out in the yard once a week to exercise and make phone calls. The only other times they could leave was to visit their lawyers or go to the infirmary.
And, with only us old guys as the exception, the cells

now held up to 30 inmates. The cells, however, were still the same 8x13 foot dimensions. The riots, if anything, had actually made things much worse.

Dr. Doolittle

In prison the weeks bled into each other. Because so little happened, you gradually lost interest in everything but your lawyer's next visit. It wasn't so much you expected him to report anything, as it was a welcome break in an otherwise unrelenting routine.

So when two doctors and a couple of nurses from the Red Cross unexpectedly showed up in the courtyard, it felt like the circus had come to town.

With very little explanation, they marched us out and had us sit in cheap red plastic chairs they had set up for us. As we were getting settled, I noticed the women prisoners, who we never ever got to see, and mentioned it to the guy next to me.
"No," he shrugged. "Faggots."

The doctors interviewed each of us "privately" and dispensed medicines from four plastic garbage bags they had brought in. They gave me a strong anti-inflammatory for my back and legs and some medicine for the "*Ochito* Weeze," my name for the wracking cough that we all share. I also scored some powdered electrolytes with soda, which worked as a stool softener.

That was enough for me. Although the real reason they had come was to give flu and tetanus shots to everyone, my needle phobia, coupled with the overall lack of hygiene in the prison, kicked in. Maybe because I had been so thankful for the medicine, they respected my wishes.

Around the same time, I got the reputation for being a healer. Because everyone was so justifiably afraid of the infirmary, prison remedies were rampant. Unfortunately, these remedies were usually just as dangerous.

I saw that first hand when Felipe went to the infirmary for an acutely inflamed navel infection. After doing nothing for five days, the infirmary gave him some cream to apply on the area. The cream, however, kept the area damp, which only worsened the infection. Deciding to trust prison folk medicine instead, he applied a paste made of garlic and milk. That, of course, only fostered the infection.

Finally, I told Felipe to clean and rinse the area with hot water as thoroughly as possible several times a day, to dry it completely, and to use some powder to keep it dry. As with most common sense solutions, it worked.

It also seemed to elevate my standing in the cell, because the inmates thought I could cure whatever ailed them. Some even started calling me *Doctor*, just because I knew how to use hydrogen peroxide and a drying agent.

Clock Without Hands -- An Interlude

I realized I passed another rite of passage when I could tell time just by listening the sounds of the prison itself.

At 5:30 in the morning, the whistle of a passing train heralded the day's beginning. Around six, a wave of what sounded like static accompanied the arrival of the morning shift. But it wasn't static; just the new shift changing stations on all the radios.

Next was the sound of breakfast being delivered down the concrete paths on flatbed carts by an armada of day workers. The gates and doors, all large, metal, and heavily barred, began clanging. And, at last, there was the noise of the cell door opening, a signal that we were free to go out into the hallway.

The tiny TV's in most of the cells started around seven in the morning and stayed on until 11 at night. Alfredo slept late, so we didn't turn the sound on in ours until about 11 o'clock in the morning, when he'd wake up. Wanting to stay on his good side, I'd watch the morning news from a San Diego news station without the sound.

Regardless of the time of day, reception was intermittent at best. The "antenna," a collage of metal and wire that hung from inside the cell across the hall and out the window, had to be in just the exact right position to produce a somewhat clear picture. Usually I could make out the English subtitles and maintain some touch with the outside world.

Later in the day, Alfredo let us watch three half-hour shows in English. The first two were old episodes of *Family Feud*, followed by 30 minutes of *Everybody Loves Chris*. *Afuera* (outside), I would have rather dumped gasoline on myself and struck a match than watch this dreck. But in prison, I became an avid fan of both.

One Chris episode opened with "Dancing with Myself." I smiled at the memories the song evoked, and fervently thanked God for all of the little things.

Unless there was a soccer game or something major, the tv was silent in the early afternoon and turned back on again in the evening. We'd start with an hour of Mexican news shows, a history or nature program originally shot in English but dubbed into Spanish, and, at seven, American shows like *CSI* and *House*, dubbed in Spanish. The best thing you can say about the tv was that it improved my Spanish; if I paid attention, I could understand most of the program.

Around 11 P.M., Alfredo, who was the only one allowed to touch the TV when he was awake, turned it off. When he did, I crawled in my bunk. Except for the sounds of prisoners being pulled out of their cell for release, which always happened after midnight, the cacophony of blaring TV's, police radios, clanging cellblock doors and metal bars, and constant conversation eventually gave way to a symphony of snores and flatulence. It was the soundtrack of old men in failing respiratory health and on a bean-based diet.

There was one other sound that happened like clockwork three times a day. It was a chant emanating from thousands of voices of the *Puro Paises* (Pure Country), which is the largest gang in the prison. Extremely active during the riots, this gang had morphed into a benign, almost religious faction.

The chant began each day at around seven, when one voice screamed *"Puro Paises,"* and was answered in kind by thousands of inmates. Then he said *"buenos dias,"* which they also repeated. At around two, the chant became *"buenos tardes,"* and at ten, *"buenas noches."* You could set your watch to it -- if you had one.

From the sounds of it, the only inmates who didn't repeat the chant are the men in my cellblock. I'm still not sure why, but suspect it's because you get over the whole gang thing when you hit 60.

No Visitors Allowed

I was lonely almost all the time but never so much as on visiting day. Early on, Carlos and I decided that the danger of someone being kidnapped and ransomed on the way to see me was too great to justify the risk. I realize that sounds paranoid, but it wasn't. No one, including the lawyers, trusted the police or the cartels that controlled so many aspects of life in Mexico.

Besides, even if they did get through safely, they'd still be subjected to the intrusive, humiliating search all visitors endure and be forced to wait for hours registering before being marched through the various locked gates and holding areas. All for a few heart breaking minutes.

If I were being totally honest, I also didn't want visitors, because I didn't want them to see me like this. That was small comfort every Saturday, though, as I watched my cellmates prepare to meet their loved ones.

From a selfish perspective, the lack of visitors also cost me all the clothes, books, food, and cups they were allowed to bring in. Visitors could have also exchanged $40 for 500 *vale* at the prison store and bought and shared the superior chicken and rice or carne asada lunches made specifically for the visiting day.

So the only visitors I got were my lawyers, who were not allowed by law to bring me anything, and seemed as frustrated by the system as I was. To their credit, they remained optimistic that the doctor's testimony and my medical records were enough to get the charges dismissed or reduced. They also assured me that something would happen within the next few weeks.

That was far preferable to going to trial, which would force me to go up against the deep-seated, pervasive anti-American feeling Mexicans have. I couldn't blame them, really, since we have screwed them at every turn, beginning from the moment we bought California, New Mexico, Arizona, Nevada,Colorado and Texas for a pittance. Santa Ana used the money to fund his war machine against the constant revolutions. It doesn't matter that he masterminded the sale. We gringos ended up taking the blame.

Make the Monkey Dance

I understand how they felt, but the Mexicans didn't have a lot of room to talk. Their treatment of foreign nationals was a clear-cut violation of international law. And the levels of prejudice on personal levels continued to shock me.

The better my Spanish got, the more I noticed the bigotry, and the more I realized they had been laughing at, not with, me. The inmates in the cell next to ours treated me like a parrot, making me repeat all kinds of ridiculous sayings. They laughed uproariously when I did, and said things about me and America that were anything but good natured.

To avoid generating more ill will, I fell into the role of the over-educated, arrogant but somehow ignorant American they expected. I pretended not to notice I was the butt of their jokes, Instead, I used it as a reminder that they would take advantage of me at every turn.

It's a fact that every American, white or black, learned to accept. Whites were *hueros* (white boys); blacks like Mingus, "niggers." Unless you were brown and a full-blooded Mexican, they didn't trust you.

Which is why you became friends with the other foreigners by default. Bob, the only other white American, and I had little in common. There's no way we'd have anything to do with each other outside. I felt the same about Eduardo, the brown man from no particular country. We wouldn't be friends *afuera*, but in there we got on famously.

Guards Just Want to Have Fun

Regardless, I'd have taken my chances with the prisoners instead of the jailers, who relished their power and didn't hesitate to exercise it randomly. One night, strictly for their own amusement, for instance, the guards roused us at midnight and had us play a twisted game of jailhouse musical chairs.

In this version, we changed cells, not chairs. Somehow, 16 guys ended up in a cell with only ten bunk beds. I got an absolutely filthy "chi chi"-infested second bunk. Luckily, I had grabbed my blankets and pillow and my medicine and food bucket. But my bathing bucket, books, and writing materials in the cell were still in the cell. I wasn't worried about my books and writing materials, which could be passed through the bars, but I wondered about the bucket.

Then I thought about all my food, my beautiful clean enclosed bunk, extra clothes, my other blanket, my toothbrush and my soap that I also left behind. It all served to remind me that I was under the thumb of a heartless, power-mad despot who liked nothing better than arbitrarily demonstrating his control.

Three hours later, the guards moved us back to our cell, where an especially filthy guy had rolled around in my bed with his shoes on. Totally disgusted, I stripped the bed and shook out the sheets. It didn't help. I felt dirty. Uncomfortable. In danger. I told myself things were going to be better, but I knew they wouldn't.

The First Cut is the Deepest

It was simply a case, I realized, of the shock of the situation was wearing off. By the end of the first month, I was acclimating to prison. All the tedium, loneliness, filth, and bleakness began to take its toll, and I slid into bouts of despair and depression. Just like everyone else around me.

It explained why most of the men slept as much of the day and night away as they could. I envied them because I had never been a good sleeper. To get to sleep, I had to drive myself into complete exhaustion every day. If I didn't, I'd toss and turn and lay awake all night, when my thoughts turned dark.

In prison, though, it was very difficult not to nap. Whenever I started to doze, I forced myself to get up and walk the ward until I was fully awake, no matter how badly it hurt.

If he was up, I'd play dominoes or chess with Mingus and talk about music, just to stay awake. Or, thanks to a box of books Mingus had stored under his bunk, at least there was something to read.

The first book I pulled out of the pile was The Rock's autobiography. I had seen him work out at Gold's a number of times. As I thought back on those times, I was reminded of how much I was missing.

The list was long, but began and ended with Nancy. On our 14th wedding anniversary, I was in jail. I wrote

Nancy a letter begging for forgiveness, but my attorneys, who I hadn't seen in four days, were the only ones who could send it. None of the books and T-shirts that they sent me a week ago had arrived, not that I expected them to. I spent the day alone, thinking about how much my actions had cost me and the people I love. I hated myself for it.

Our anniversary was traditionally the start of the family Thanksgiving celebration, so my mood got bleaker day by day. It didn't help that several days before, out of the blue, Mingus got his release order. Two hours later, after giving me the books and the chess set, he was gone.

Although I was glad for him, I was also devastated. He was my best friend, my chess and domino partner, and my mentor. He taught me how to survive in this evil place, and our mutual love of music made the day more tolerable. For me, it was an incalculable loss.

My court date was supposed to be the next day. I fantasized about being released too, but the day dragged on without any sign of that happening. Since it was the one day a week I could go into the yard, I dragged myself to the phone banks and called my two older sisters, Jan and Ann.
Jan was never judgmental, so she was easy to speak. Ann, on the other hand, was constantly preaching about "my evil ways." I would suffer through her diatribe, because it was heartfelt and because she was entirely in the right.

Collectively we decided to shut my youngest sister,

Linda, out of the loop, because we didn't think she could keep it from my 86-year-old mother. But we also knew we were not going to be able to keep it secret much longer

Next I called Michael Sullivan, a friend who was helping with the Cyndi Lauper shoot. He told me that they were start shooting next week in Memphis. I had really wanted to be there for it. I still hadn't talked to Cyndi. I was afraid this would ruin my relationship with her. It's not like I could blame her.

Michael had more important things to tell me. He had talked to Carlos, who told him that my hearing was going on. They didn't need me to testify, so there was no reason for me to be there.

The hearing, he explained, was strictly concerned with my medical records, which detailed my treatment for PTSD, my prescription drug history (including Soma), and the spine-stem stimulator implant. Carlos had had these records notarized, sent from LA and translated into Spanish.

To sweeten the report, the Tijuana doctor, who wrote me the prescription and saw me at the prison, was on my side and the chief medical authority the court would hear from.

To further cheer me up, he told me that one of my favorite teams, LSU, had beat rival Ole Miss in the last minute to remain 10 and 1. And my favorite team, Super Bowl Champion New Orleans Saints, were still in the running for the playoffs.

The next day, Carlos finally came. He handed me an especially gratifying note from Nancy, who told me she loved me. It was great to hear but consumed me with guilt. Because of me, she had to give notice on our place and move to somewhere cheaper. She didn't complain, but I knew she was worried about the move's effects on our youngest dog, Roo, who was ill, and our other pets. As the extent of my screw up became more apparent, I wondered how I'd ever forgive myself again.

Before leaving me to my thoughts, Carlos repeated that he hoped I'd be out within the month. While there were no guarantees, he thought there was a 90% chance things would go our way.

Despite all his assurances, I couldn't get to sleep that night. All I could think about is how nothing had gone right since I got to Mexico. I saw no reason to believe that streak was going to change.

The other inmates backed me up on that. They kept telling me that no one got out that quickly. "Once you're in, you're in." They used Mingus, who was in here for well over a year before his release, as a case in point.

I was most worried about a discrepancy in the doctor's report. He claimed he prescribed me 200 mg Somas, but the ones I had bought were 350 mg. Carlos didn't think the judge would notice. But since it had been the bumbling prison doctor, Dr. Narango, who discovered the difference, I wasn't as optimistic. If he could spot it, I reasoned, anyone could. Carlos tried to calm me down by pointing out that Somas weren't even illegal in

Mexico, and that I had been more a target of an extortion plot than anything else.

The only thing that helped lift my funk was a string of holiday football games on television. We watched a really good NFL game between the Green Bay Packers and the Atlanta Falcons, who won on a last second field goal. During the game, they showed highlights of the Saints/Dallas game from Thanksgiving Day. The Saints won 30-27 after Dallas missed a last second field goal. Even in prison, Sunday morning is unusually quiet, so my screaming and cheering throughout the game seemed deafening.

As the holiday weekend droned on, I had a moment of clarity. "I am here because of my drug use," I told myself. "I am not a victim, and the accident and pain are not valid justification for the price the drugs are extracting on me and my family. It's a little late in coming, but I no longer want to go through life sedated. I want that part of my life to be over. " I promised myself it would.

Thanksgiving was just the beginning of a parade of family events, including the birthdays of Billy, Dan, and my youngest grandson, Will. All would go on without me. Then, just as the self-pity was cresting, Carlos told me that we were getting close.

The D.A. had just 72 hours to either present new evidence against me or dispute the evidence that had been presented. Since all the evidence suggested the pills were for legal, personal use, not distribution, he expected the ruling to go our way. But, he warned me,

"Quien sabe?" (who knows?).

Let's Go Crazy

All I could do was pray and trust in God that all would go well. If it didn't, I'd be in here for years. When I pictured that, my thoughts turned as black as the insects and rodents that infest this place. I revisit the idea of suicide, finding the idea of regaining control over my own destiny exhilarating. But, thinking of what that would do to my family, I grimly resolve to survive.

Although it sounds like an oxymoron, I stayed sane by walking the ward and escaping into my past and a world of my own making. It was an insanity of its own, but it was also the only way I could deal with the oppressive uncertainty weighing down on me.

It wasn't like I had a lot of tools at my disposal. The entire sum of my weekly activities could be summarized in a short list: a bath every other day, laundry every third, cleaning, the occasional visit to the *locutorio* to see my attorneys, and watching television, reading, and trying to write or study my Spanish.

With so little to do, I was left alone with my thoughts and my anxiety most of the time. Walking the ward, saying a mantra (usually a Rosary), and slipping into a totally meditative state was my only way of passing the time.

When I had gotten to prison, I had fallen back into the flashbacks that had plagued me since the crash. Sometimes there would be flaming friends and family, sometimes not. There was always a burning plane.

The longer I played with these meditative states, the more control I gained over the flashbacks. I learned how to shift topics, which made it a much more effective escape mechanism.

I knew I was toying with madness, but it was a much better place than my reality. So I'd spend each day gimping up and down the tunnel, muttering in a trance, lost in my dream world. That, combined with all the books and the writings, gave me a mystical air. No longer did the inmates think of me as *El Doctor*. Now I was *El Professor*.

I have to admit, there was something mystical about walking the ward every day. The walls and bars would melt, and I'd slip into a state that was simultaneously life-like and dreamy. It was like having a private music video channel wired directly to my brain, starring me, every woman I had ever been attracted to, and every memory of the rock world my brain could access.

The better I got at it, the more I realized it was my plan B. If I couldn't get out of prison, I would enter a world of my own construction. In other words, I'd get released or go crazy. It was the only way to escape from this place any time you wanted.

Resolution Day

Several weeks later, I got the notice that my fate was going to be resolved, one way or another, within 24 hours. Having waited so long, I didn't know what to expect. I only knew I'd be strong enough to deal with it, however it went down.

To pass the time, I read the last book left in Mingus' stash, Shakespeare's *The Tempest*. When Trinculo, seeking shelter from the storm, finds Caliban the monster, shares his coat and says, "Misery acquaints a man with strange bedfellows," I felt that he was talking directly to me.

Whatever hopes of staying upbeat and optimistic were shattered at six in the morning, when the guards dragged me out of bed, walked me through the prison to the holding cell in the courtyard and took me to the infirmary. After the doctor said I was in good enough shape to be moved, we walked around the prison some more, collecting the other prisoners who were going with us.

By the time they shoved 20 of us into a 10-seat van, I was already in pain. They drove to the Federal Building at the usual bone-breaking speed and then left us in the hot sun in the locked vehicle for more than an hour. By the time they came back, my legs were so bad that I fell twice and had to be helped up by another inmate.
The holding cells were packed as usual, but the guards, aware of my physical problems, put me with the women prisoners in a small cell. A plexi-glass divider separated it from an office with a court reporter, the judge's assistant, and the lawyers, who for the most part ignored us.

Several hours later, they moved us to a different room that looked exactly like the other one, except for the steady stream of prisoners coming in and out.

Some of these guys looked really bad. Three particularly threatening gangbangers, clearly cartel assassins, were charged with the murder of several policemen. Inside the cell, they openly bragged about the killings. In front of the judge, though, they vehemently protested their innocence.

After waiting for hours, I got all of five minutes with a judge's assistant and Carlos, who were both protected by a thick plexiglass window. I tried to butter the assistant up by calling her *Senorita Bonita* (pretty woman), but she was having none of that.

She brusquely told me that they had received my medical records from the U.S. and translated them into Spanish. She also said that they had located the doctor who gave me the prescription but warned me not to put too much hope in his testimony, because the Tijuana police were pressing for a maximum sentence. Then, in a line that still rings in my ears, she told me that they'd soon decide whether to set me free or imprison me for the next five to ten years.

Neither Carlos, who I could only communicate with via hand signals, nor I barely said a word. With Senorita Bonita's warning floating around my head, I left there in the worst pain and in the blackest of moods.

They then took me back to the original holding cell and then, around 5:30, back to my old cell. I hadn't eaten all day and was distraught. I couldn't help think that no matter what evidence we presented them with, I was going to be here for some time. From what I had already seen and been through, I knew it was akin to a death sentence. I would not leave the prison alive.

Thirty minutes later, depressed beyond belief, I was shocked when a day worker came to the cellblock door and escorted me to the *Locutorio*. I figured it was my attorneys, coming in with a pep talk, but it was a court official, telling me that I was going to be released that night.

She told me that the Tijuana police had been so confident of my conviction that the prosecution lawyers hadn't even bothered to show up. Shocked and upset with the verdict, they planned on doing everything they could to keep me from crossing that border to America.

Even that didn't damper the emotional relief flooding my body. I kissed a day worker on the cheek, telling the woman behind the thick plexi-glass the kiss was for her. And since I wasn't going to need them anymore, I gave the worker a few hundred *vale*.

When I got back to the cell and told the other inmates the news, everyone seemed happy for me, because it gave them hope too. I took what I hoped would be my last bucket bath and put on the clothes I had been arrested in. I distributed the rest of my *vale* and my personal possessions to the guys who needed them the most or who had been the most friendly.

The unadulterated joy the gift brought them was overwhelming. I was giving away something that was worthless to me, but life changing for them. I hope I never forget how that type of random act of kindness can change the attitude of so many. Then I began counting the minutes until midnight, and freedom.

It's Not Over 'Til It's Over

As the day dragged on, I couldn't shake images of the police were gunning for me, or being turned out into the cold, rainy night 15 miles from the border, with no money, no identification, no access to my attorneys, and very little chance of actually getting to the border. The inmates assured me I was worried about nothing, but I didn't believe them.

Eventually, sometime after midnight, the officials came and got me from the cell. Once again we did the walking around thing. I was led past several other prisoners who were also being released and literally thrown into the back of a van. I was sure they were going to hand me over to the Tijuana police, who would throw me into their jail, torture me, and then extort a ransom from my family for my release.

Ten minutes later, prison guards walked me into another institutional building. I was processed by the Tijuana police, which scared the hell out of me, and put in yet another cell.

But to my astonishment, this cell was big and fairly clean. There were only three other inmates in it, all of whom were sleeping soundly. The bathroom, which had an actual shower, hot and cold running water, and a door, was an even greater shock. Seeing it, I regretted enduring that last bucket bath.

A policeman handed me a couple of blankets that were wrapped in plastic and a similarly wrapped pillow, and pointed me to a four-inch covered mattress. Rather than sleep, I spent the rest of the night with my back against the wall, thinking I was being softened up for the kill.

Around 9am, as the prison came to life and the three other prisoners woke up, I was still pressed against the concrete wall. When I asked them where I was, I was surprised to find out they were Guatemalans who were caught passing through Mexico (illegally) on their way to the States (illegally).

They told me that I was in Immigration and scheduled for deportation. I still didn't really believe them, but sometime after a breakfast of real eggs, real bacon, real coffee, and milk, I understood that I was in the hands of the Federal Government, who were protecting me from the Tijuana Police.

To their credit, that protection included escorting me out of the country.

The guards, who were friendlier than any I had come across, let me use the pay phone. By now, I had memorized the landline numbers and called Cholly in Seattle, who had more or less been my point man with Carlos.

His daughter, Emily, was the only one at home. She called my family and my attorneys, who didn't know I had been released. (I later found out that Carlos has come to Immigration as soon as he heard I was there, but they wouldn't let him see me.)

Finally, around three in the afternoon, two days before Christmas, I was handcuffed and shackled for the ride that I hoped was to the border. As always, they drove at very high speeds, with all the lights flashing. At the border, handcuffed and shackled, I was transferred to an American border agent.

"Am I on American soil?" I asked him.

"Yes," he answered.

Without thinking, in an act that you've seen many times before, I dropped down and kissed the ground. I would have kissed him too if I didn't think he'd take it the right way.

I told him very briefly about what had happened to me in Mexico, a place I once loved. He looked at me, said "Mexico is no longer a place for Americans," and led me off to be processed.

I didn't know what to expect from the processing, since I had no identification on me. But all they asked for was my name and social security number, so they could see if I had any outstanding warrants. Then I was pointed to the oddly named WOP line, which in this world is an abbreviation for "without papers."

I was the only WOP, which shortened the four hour wait to minutes. When I looked up, I couldn't believe my eyes. Carlos was waiting for me there in the U.S. with a copy of my passport.

Evidently, he had made quite a fuss to insure that my re-entry was easy. Whatever he did worked, for I was out of there in less than a minute. When I walked through, I could see him crying.

Emotionally burnt and numb, I stepped out of the Customs area and into the late afternoon Southern California light. My son-in-law picked me up and took me to his and my daughter's home in North County, San Diego. I don't think he saw the tears, but, then again, I truly didn't care. I was home. I was free.

EPILOGUE

I sit alone in a darkened house, the only light emanating from my computer screen, this Halloween, the 31st of October, 2013, I hear the neighborhood children laugh as they wander down the sidewalk. I am humbled by the love and light that surrounds me. And although I'm no expert, I'm starting to get an idea how redemption feels.

EPILOGUE
Redux

I lay alone in a darkened room. The sole illumination comes from the monitors and the array of medical technology surrounding me.

Three days ago I was diagnosed with CLL, Chronic lymphocytic leukemia and rushed to the Emergency Room. Now, as poisonous chemo drugs drip into me, I wonder whether I will live or die. I fully expect to get out of this bed and back to the gym but, if it's the latter, I'm completely okay and at peace with that.

For it has been my experience that we, as flawed human beings, constantly move in and out of the light. Our job is to navigate towards it to the best of our abilities. Although I'm constantly falling short, I am trying like hell. I believe that matters.

So does the one thought that constantly loops inside of my head as I lay here. Come what may, it's not enough to strive to live in the light. You must try to die in it, also.

Peace - Santa Monica Hospital, July 11, 2015.

APPENDIX : MY PRISON FAMILY

1. Alfredo Velasquez: Alfredo, who had the middle bunk directly across from me, had been in for more than three years. He had an aristocratic bearing, was one of the few inmates who read something other than the Bible, spoke a little English, and was teaching himself German. He was also the only other inmate to exercise, and started joining me when I'd use things in our cell like water bottles for weights. He was in for what I assumed was murder or manslaughter, but was always impeccably groomed, and ran the cell.

2. Bodelo Andrado: He was in the bunk beneath me. For no real reason, I didn't get along with him. I believe he was in prison because of some morals charge, and was probably a pedophile. A defrocked priest, he spent his entire day copying passages out of the Bible.

3. Eduardo Flores: He slept in the middle back bunk, claimed he was a U.S. citizen of Latin descent, and lived in Santa Monica, less than a mile from my home. His wife worked at the 99 Cent store, and spoke no English. His was passable, but he could barely read or write either English or Spanish. He had a son by a Norwegian woman who lived with him. He worked for AT&T, and seemed to be a man without a first language or a country. He was the only person in our cell who had a visitor: his wife, who would take a 4 A.M. bus from Santa Monica all the way to Tijuana almost every Sunday. I believe he was in for a morals charge, although I couldn't tell you why.

4. Pancho Mendoza: Pancho had the single bed in

front of the little dividing wall next to the bathroom. A truck driver for the cartels, he was busted with several tons of pot and insisted he was set up by a competing cartel. Big and loud, he was Alfredo's man and did as he was told. He actually offered me a job driving for the cartel when I got out. He thought they'd love a 60-year-old American driving for them.

5. Felipe Lucatella: Occupying the bottom back bunk directly below Eduardo, he was a day worker who spent 14 hours a day getting things for the inmates. Also a trucker, he was serving a ten-year stretch for hauling pot, which he admitted guilt for, and an 18-year sentence for weapons, which he accused the police of planting. I believed him.

6. Humberto Guerrero: He had the middle bunk on the right side of the cell, but when he saw how difficult it was for me to walk and would have problems getting into the top bunk, he offered to change bunks. It was a lifesaver. He spoke very good English and had kids, American citizens, who lived in L.A. We quickly became friends, Taking me under his wing, he showed me the ropes of prison. He looked very young, probably because he was really only 47 and had lied to get into *Tecero Edad*.

He also was the only prisoner in my cell to be released after my arrival. When he left he gave me a notebook, which I used to write all this. In the back of the notebook, I found a letter to his wife, much like the one I had written to Nancy, promising he would change his evil ways.

Since he had been in prison on both sides of the

border more times than he could count, I seriously doubted it.

7. Antonio Rodriguez: A genuine have not, Antonio occupied the back top bunk, and was pretty weird and extremely quiet. I suspected that he was in for burglary, felt sorry for him, and slipped him whatever leftovers I may have. I only had one real conversation with him. Despite not knowing a word of English, he walked up to me and sang the Allman Brother's song, "One Way Out," perfectly. He told me it was a song by his favorite band, ZZ Top. I didn't correct him.

8. Robert McClements: The only other caucasian American in the cell, he had the bottom bunk across from me, directly below Alfredo. He was a 73-year-old meth addict, and was totally estranged from his only family, two daughters, who were leaving him in prison to rot. He was in prison because he had driven south on the 405 from his home in Long Beach, not stopping until he crashed into the concrete barriers of the Mexican border.

Sickly and prone to dizzy spells and seizures, he was an extremely difficult man. His bail had been set at $1800, which he claimed he had, but no one from the States cared enough to get it to him. I felt sorry for him too, even though he seemed content to be in here with no responsibilities to bother him.

9. Jose Luis Pardo: Another quiet guy, he bunked above Alfredo. I don't remember ever speaking to him.

10. Antonio Rodriguez: Another have not, Antonio replaced Humberto in the bunk above me. He and his

brother, who was in another cell, had been busted on some drug charge or another. He worked for me for *vale*, but I never really got to know him.

Ochito

11. Angel: Angel was a gangbanger I met in the Federal building lock up and who went to *La Pinta* the day before I did. Tattooed head to foot, he was accomplished in mixed martial arts, and was an assassin for a cartel, with at least seven kills to his credit. He told me that there were at least two more, which was why he was in there.

12. Huero: The nickname meant "white boy," which seemed to fit since he was a Mexican with blue eyes and light skin. He worked for the cartels smuggling one and a half tons of pot at a time in a Winnebago. He was sure the cartel would either spring him or, because he knew so much about their operation, kill him.

He spoke excellent English and was the cell leader for my first three days in *Ochito*. He was very friendly and protective of me, making sure I got a bunk even though I had walked into an overcrowded cell. In a random act of kindness, he wrote me a little note to remain hopeful when I was at a low point. It read:

John Diaz, How are you? It's me, Huero. Hopefully you leave here soon because you are a white ass friend. It doesn't matter if you use the pills but you deserve to be with your family. God bless you my friend. I am in building 1 Pasillo A cell 201. Whenever you want to write, you know you have a friend here and hopefully we leave soon to be united with our family. I seen you Mon. sitting in the patio, I was really glad to see you. -- Huero

I remain grateful for that note to this day.

13. Marco: A Mexican who spent most of his time across the border. He was in for a knife charge, but made bail and had the charges dropped within three days. Claiming to have had a professional boxing career, he and I would entertain the others by shadow boxing and slap fighting. He said he was going to make a comeback in the ring, but after holding my own against him, I recommended sticking to his day job as a car mechanic.

14/15. Juan and his cousin: Juan was a heavy set Mexican in his late 20s who was in and out of *La Pinta* for manufacturing and distributing meth. He was in with his cousin, who was supposedly the brains of the operation. Since they were constantly in prison, brains may have been an exaggeration.

Be that as it may, Juan had spent a lot of time in the U.S., spoke excellent English, and was with me when I was processed into the system. He was the one who told me about *Tercero Edad*, and shepherded me through the long processing procedures, so I owe him a huge debt of gratitude. My lot would have been much, much worse had he not been there.

Other People of Note in "Tercero Edad

16. Eugene Mingus: Eugene was a black American and son of jazz great, Charlie Mingus, whom I had once met in the late 70s at an Earth, Wind and Fire concert. The only African American in the cellblock, he was a victim of frequent racist behavior. Although he was called "nigger" all the time, though, he didn't seem to be that bothered about it. The only racists to worry about, he said, were the smart ones, and none of them were here.

Easily my best friend in *La Pinta*, he was busted in Tijuana for growing exotic marijuana. All the other prisoners said they saw it on TV when he got busted. His sudden release came as a total surprise, since he hadn't even spoken to his attorney for months.

17. Hector Galaviz: A day worker in prison processing, Hector spoke great English, fingerprinted the new inmates, and had unparalleled access to the prison store, which is how he earned his keep. I think he was in for drugs and pills. He told me I would never get out of *La Pinta*.

18. Marco Antonio Contraras: An extremely clever handy man, he made my stinger, my pillow, and the curtains which enclosed my bunk. He was in for murder but found out that the "Federales" were dropping the homicide case against him because the gun, which the police said they found at the crime scene, didn't match the weapon that killed the individual.

Despite that, the state is trying to keep him here on a bogus charge. Prior to the case being dropped, he had sworn to me that he was innocent of the crime he was accused of -- but that he was a hit man and a gangbanger who had killed many people.

19: Effron Magana: Effron, who spoke passable English and knew a lot about classic Rock & Roll, had worked for John Huston in Will Roger's old Pacific Palisades house (currently Will Rogers State Park). When I was being processed, he was the smoker who told me to make sure I asked for the *Tercero Edad*. He also helped me through my last day and through my "resolution." As with so many others, I might not have made it through without him.

About the Authors

John Diaz

John Diaz has been at the epicenters of contemporary music, media, and entertainment since Woodstock, where he talked his way into becoming a stage manager, all the way through a storied role in the rise of the music video, the development of the concert film for television and the big screen, and the dawn of the digital revolution. He has worked extensively with virtually every musical legend, including Bruce Springsteen, Bob Dylan, Michael Jackson, the Allman Brothers, ZZ Top, and Sting. He is married to the artist, Nancy Louise Jones. This is his first book.

Neil Feineman

Neil Feineman has written for and edited music journalism for many years, including three magazines he co-founded, Beach Culture, Raygun, and Revolution. He has written numerous books, such as 30 Frames per Second: The Art of the Music Video (with Steve Reiss) and Geek Chic, and collaborated with Sigur Ros on the privately published, In a Frozen Sea. Most recently he wrote all the text for the exhibit, Spectacle, devoted to the art, history, and state of the music video, currently at the EMP in Seattle, Washington.

The Authors would like to acknowledge the following:

My family has always stayed beside me, and I love them. I know how lucky I am to have them.

My biggest hero will always and forever be, my wife, Nancy Louise Jones. She stuck with me when most would have walked, and has supported me in some extremely gnarly situations.

As in any fable, there are many heroes to acknowledge. Carlos Garcia, his partner and his legal team certainly are heroes by any definition. My great friends, Cholly Mercer and William Broad, both moved heaven and earth to facilitate my release and have my undying friendship and love.

My cousin, Brian Diaz, deserves an award for coming over to Taiwan to get me after the accident. Theresa Poy, my assistant after the crash, never gave up on me, and was the motivating force to getting the operation, which freed me from wheelchairs and crutches and started me walking again. Lisa Nunziela, who diligently typed all of my hand written notes and was a motivating force in this tome. Dr. Bernard M. Bierman, MD, Dr. Susan Smalley, who recommended the amazing Dr. Laura Audell, who oversaw my physical recovery and continues to do so.

I also want to thank my close friends Dan Nunenmacher, Rob Faust, Tom Argote, Rob Tonkin, David Doyle, Hudson Marquez, Sandy DeSoto, Andy Morahan, Eric Mitchell, Franc. Reyes, Lauren Sinclair, Art Stevens, Jackie Kain, Cyndi Lauren, Tony Dimitriades and Kevin Wall. Professionals, Dr.Tom Baholyodin, MD, and Dr. Paul

Oberon, PHD.   All the guys and gals at Gold's Gym deserve a shout out, also.

Finally my co-writer, Neil Feineman, took approximately 600,000 words scribbled in journals, on toilet paper and many other scraps and pieces of written material, to form a cohesive tale, and then to re-write it so that it somehow sounded more like my own voice than that which I originally wrote.

There are many others that could and should be acknowledged here, but any of you that I may have forgotten, please remember that you live in my heart and I am deeply appreciative of your support.   You have no idea how much it has helped.

www.caughtupinthefable.com